I0012539

BGP: The Protocol that Connects the Internet

James Relington

DEDICATION

To those who seek knowledge, inspiration, and new perspectives—
may this book be a companion on your journey, a spark for curiosity,
and a reminder that every page turned is a step toward discovery.

The Origins of BGP 9

BGP and the Birth of the Modern Internet 12

Understanding Autonomous Systems 15

The Evolution from EGP to BGP 18

BGP Versions: From 1 to 4 21

How BGP Works at a High Level 24

The BGP Finite State Machine 28

Peering Agreements and Relationships......................................31

Internal vs. External BGP..34

BGP Route Selection Process..38

BGP Attributes Explained 41

The Role of AS_PATH...45

The Power of LOCAL_PREF...48

MED and Inter-AS Path Selection 51

BGP Next Hop Attribute...54

The Importance of BGP Communities 58

BGP Confederations 61

Route Reflectors and iBGP Scaling 65

BGP and Policy Control...68

BGP Filtering Techniques...72

Prefix Lists and Route Maps 75

The BGP Decision Process in Depth...78

BGP and Multi-Homing...82

BGP and Traffic Engineering..85

BGP Route Aggregation..89

BGP and MPLS VPNs 92

The Role of BGP in Data Centers..96

BGP and Cloud Networking..99

BGP Security: Threats and Risks...103

The Impact of BGP Hijacking 106

BGP Monitoring and Logging...110

BGP Best Practices 113

BGP Troubleshooting Techniques...117

Case Studies of BGP Incidents 120

BGP and Internet Exchange Points...123

Understanding BGP Flap Dampening 127

Graceful Restart and BGP..130

BGP Route Refresh Capability 133

BGP and IPv6...136

Segment Routing and BGP...140

The Role of BGP in SDN 143

BGP in Content Delivery Networks 147

BGP for DDoS Mitigation 150

BGP and Anycast Deployments...153

BGP and Network Automation 157

Open Source BGP Implementations 160

Vendor-Specific BGP Features..164

The Future of BGP 168

Regulatory and Compliance Considerations 171

BGP and the Global Routing Table...174

BGP in Satellite and Edge Networks..177

The Unseen Backbone: BGP and Everyday Life 181

AKNOWLEDGEMENTS

I would like to express my deepest gratitude to everyone who contributed to the creation of this book. To my colleagues and mentors, your insights and expertise have been invaluable. A special thank you to my family and friends for their unwavering support and encouragement throughout this journey.

The Origins of BGP

The story of the Border Gateway Protocol, commonly known as BGP, is intertwined with the very fabric of the modern Internet. Its origins can be traced back to a time when the Internet was still a nascent and experimental network, largely confined to academic institutions and government agencies. During the 1980s, the primary routing protocol in use was the Exterior Gateway Protocol, or EGP. EGP, however, was limited in scope and design. It could only operate within a hierarchical network structure, making it inadequate for the rapidly expanding and diversifying Internet of the time.

As more organizations and networks sought to connect to the Internet, a more robust and scalable solution became necessary. The limitations of EGP became evident as the need for a more dynamic and decentralized routing system grew. EGP lacked the flexibility to handle multiple autonomous systems interacting on a peer-to-peer basis, which was quickly becoming the reality of the burgeoning Internet. These limitations sparked the search for a new protocol, one capable of addressing the challenges of this new era of interconnected networks.

In 1989, a group of engineers, including Yakov Rekhter from IBM and Kirk Lougheed from Cisco, took on the task of designing what would eventually become BGP. Their work was driven by the growing need for a protocol that could scale alongside the exponential growth of the Internet and support the increasingly complex policies of independent networks. The protocol had to be capable of managing how autonomous systems, or ASes, exchanged routing information. This would enable networks to make independent policy decisions while maintaining global connectivity.

The initial draft of BGP was documented in Request for Comments (RFC) 1105, which was published in June 1989. This early version of BGP was intended as a stopgap solution, a way to replace EGP and provide a more flexible routing system for the short term. However, as the Internet continued to grow and evolve, BGP proved to be more than just a temporary fix. It became the de facto standard for inter-domain routing, responsible for holding together the increasingly vast and complex web of networks that make up the Internet.

One of the key design principles behind BGP was its focus on policy-based routing. Unlike EGP, which prioritized a hierarchical structure, BGP allowed individual autonomous systems to define their own routing policies. This flexibility enabled networks to control the selection of routes based on a variety of attributes, such as path length, origin, and local preferences. BGP introduced the concept of the AS_PATH attribute, which helped prevent routing loops by keeping track of the autonomous systems a route had traversed. This mechanism not only enhanced the stability of the Internet but also gave operators the tools they needed to shape and influence traffic flows according to their own business or technical requirements.

Throughout the early 1990s, BGP continued to evolve. The protocol underwent several iterations, leading to the introduction of BGP-4, the version that is still widely used today. BGP-4, specified in RFC 4271, introduced support for Classless Inter-Domain Routing (CIDR), which was a crucial development for addressing the problem of IPv4 address exhaustion. CIDR allowed for more efficient allocation of IP addresses and helped reduce the size of global routing tables, making Internet routing more scalable.

BGP's development and adoption were not without challenges. The early Internet community had to contend with issues of interoperability, security, and reliability. However, through collaboration and constant refinement, BGP matured into a protocol capable of supporting the explosive growth of the Internet throughout the 1990s and into the 21st century. As commercial entities began connecting to the Internet, BGP played a pivotal role in enabling the emergence of a competitive, multi-provider ecosystem. The protocol allowed different Internet service providers (ISPs) to interconnect, negotiate peering agreements, and exchange routing information in a way that fostered both competition and resilience.

BGP's significance became even more apparent during key moments in the history of the Internet. For example, during periods of major outages or disruptions, BGP's behavior and the policies set by network operators often determined how traffic was rerouted and how quickly services could be restored. The decentralized nature of BGP has been both a strength and a vulnerability, enabling independent decision-making while also being susceptible to misconfigurations and malicious activities such as route hijacking.

Despite its age, BGP has proven remarkably adaptable. Over the decades, it has been extended and enhanced to support new technologies and architectures, from VPNs and MPLS networks to the integration of IPv6 and advances in data center networking. The protocol's extensibility has ensured its continued relevance in a rapidly changing technological landscape.

At its core, BGP is a testament to the collaborative spirit and ingenuity of the early Internet pioneers. What began as a modest solution to the limitations of EGP has become the foundational protocol that connects the globe. Every email sent, every website accessed, and every video streamed across the Internet today relies, at some level, on the routing decisions made by BGP. Its legacy is woven into the very infrastructure that powers modern communication, commerce, and culture.

As we look back at the origins of BGP, it becomes clear that its story is one of evolution and adaptation. From its inception in a small group of engineers tackling the challenges of a young Internet to its status today as the backbone of global interconnectivity, BGP's journey mirrors that of the Internet itself—growing, adapting, and overcoming obstacles to link people and networks around the world.

BGP and the Birth of the Modern Internet

The Border Gateway Protocol, or BGP, did not just emerge as another networking protocol; it played a pivotal role in shaping what we now recognize as the modern Internet. In the early days of networking, the Internet was a relatively small collection of interconnected systems, primarily used by research institutions, universities, and government bodies. Communication between these networks was facilitated by the Exterior Gateway Protocol (EGP), which served its purpose when the Internet's topology was still simple and hierarchical. However, as the 1990s approached, it became increasingly evident that the Internet was evolving into something much larger, more complex, and global in scale. The rigid, tree-like structure enforced by EGP could no longer support the diversity of emerging networks that wanted to interconnect on their own terms.

BGP was designed to solve this problem by enabling a decentralized, policy-based approach to inter-domain routing. The introduction of BGP allowed networks, referred to as autonomous systems (ASes), to make independent decisions regarding how they routed traffic to and from other networks. This autonomy was essential to the commercial and competitive spirit that began to define the Internet during the 1990s. Rather than relying on a centralized routing system that dictated a single path for traffic, BGP gave each network operator the freedom to establish peering relationships and routing policies that suited their specific needs and business models.

The shift from a government-controlled research network to a dynamic, commercially driven Internet was fueled in part by BGP's ability to facilitate such flexible interconnections. The early adoption of BGP by Internet service providers (ISPs) and backbone networks enabled the rise of multiple competing providers, each managing their own segment of the Internet while still contributing to global connectivity. This distributed model allowed for redundancy and resilience, features that were critical as the Internet transitioned from a niche academic tool to an indispensable platform for global communication and commerce.

During the early to mid-1990s, BGP's role became even more pronounced as the Internet underwent rapid commercialization. The National Science Foundation Network (NSFNET), which had acted as the de facto backbone for much of the United States' Internet traffic, was decommissioned. In its place, private backbone providers stepped in, creating a mesh of interconnected networks. BGP made this transition possible by providing the routing protocol that would allow disparate providers to exchange routing information in a standardized and efficient manner. Without BGP, the fragmented landscape of private networks would have struggled to operate cohesively, stalling the Internet's global expansion.

The impact of BGP on the birth of the modern Internet extends beyond technical considerations; it also enabled the development of the peering and transit agreements that underpin today's Internet economics. Autonomous systems could choose whether to establish peering relationships, exchanging traffic without payment, or purchase transit services from upstream providers. This freedom of choice fueled competition among ISPs, drove innovation in routing technologies, and gave rise to the complex web of business relationships that sustain the Internet today. BGP's policy-based routing capabilities allowed each network to enforce business-driven decisions directly in the routing process, further solidifying its importance to the evolving Internet economy.

BGP's influence also extended to the architecture of Internet Exchange Points (IXPs), which became critical hubs where networks could interconnect and exchange traffic efficiently. The growth of IXPs helped localize traffic flows, reduce costs, and improve latency, all while relying on BGP as the protocol to share routing information among participants. This evolution significantly improved the performance and scalability of the Internet, enabling it to support a growing number of users and applications. The shift toward regional and local peering at IXPs demonstrated how BGP empowered networks to optimize their traffic and minimize dependency on long-haul transit providers.

Throughout this period, BGP was not simply a passive component; it actively shaped how the Internet was built and operated. As the World Wide Web emerged and exploded in popularity during the mid-to-late 1990s, BGP silently worked behind the scenes, facilitating the rapid exchange of routing information between countless networks across continents. This seamless interconnection allowed websites, applications, and services to be accessible to users worldwide, regardless of the physical location of servers or users. The universality of BGP ensured that an ISP in Europe could easily exchange routes with a provider in Asia or North America, maintaining the truly global nature of the Internet.

While the technical specifications of BGP might seem abstract to non-specialists, its role in enabling the modern, commercial Internet cannot be overstated. Every time a user accesses an online service, sends an email, or streams media, BGP is responsible for guiding that data through a complex maze of autonomous systems. Each AS makes routing decisions based on its policies and relationships, all coordinated via BGP to maintain the global connectivity that billions of people rely on daily.

As the Internet grew in both size and complexity, so too did the challenges associated with managing and securing BGP. Yet, its core principles—flexibility, autonomy, and scalability—have remained remarkably consistent since its inception. Even as new technologies such as Content Delivery Networks (CDNs), cloud computing, and edge networking have emerged, BGP continues to serve as the routing foundation beneath them.

The birth of the modern Internet was not the result of a single technological breakthrough, but rather the combination of several critical developments, with BGP standing out as one of the most influential. By enabling the Internet to break free from the limitations of hierarchical routing and central control, BGP helped give rise to a decentralized, resilient, and rapidly expanding network that has transformed every aspect of modern life. Its legacy is reflected in the countless networks and systems that now span the globe, all speaking the common language of BGP to keep the digital world connected.

Understanding Autonomous Systems

To fully grasp how the Internet functions on a global scale, one must first understand the concept of autonomous systems, or ASes. At the heart of Internet routing and interconnectivity, autonomous systems are the building blocks that form the decentralized structure of the modern Internet. Each AS is a network, or a collection of IP prefixes, that operates under a single administrative domain and follows a unified routing policy. Autonomous systems range from small Internet service providers and universities to large multinational corporations and vast Tier 1 backbone networks that span continents. Despite the diversity of their size and purpose, they all share a common characteristic: the ability to make independent routing decisions.

Autonomous systems are identified by unique numerical identifiers called Autonomous System Numbers, or ASNs. These numbers are assigned by regional Internet registries such as ARIN, RIPE NCC, APNIC, LACNIC, and AFRINIC. ASNs are essential for distinguishing one AS from another within the global routing system. Originally, ASNs were 16-bit numbers, which allowed for approximately 65,000 unique identifiers. However, as the number of networks grew rapidly, the Internet Engineering Task Force (IETF) introduced 32-bit ASNs to accommodate the increasing demand, significantly expanding the pool of available AS numbers.

The fundamental role of an autonomous system is to manage routing within its own network, as well as to participate in routing with external networks. Inside an AS, routing is typically handled by Interior Gateway Protocols (IGPs) such as OSPF, IS-IS, or EIGRP. These protocols are responsible for determining the optimal paths between routers within the same administrative domain. However, when traffic needs to be exchanged between different autonomous systems, Border Gateway Protocol (BGP) takes over. BGP is the protocol that connects these otherwise independent networks, allowing them to share reachability information and establish paths for data to travel across the broader Internet.

The concept of autonomy is crucial to understanding why ASes are so important. Each AS has complete control over how it handles routing internally and how it communicates externally. This autonomy allows networks to implement their own policies, optimize performance, and prioritize business interests. For instance, one AS might choose to prefer traffic through a specific peer due to cost savings, while another might route traffic through a different provider to reduce latency. These routing policies are implemented and enforced through BGP, making the interplay between ASes a complex, dynamic, and constantly evolving process.

Autonomous systems can be classified into different types depending on their function and position in the global Internet hierarchy. Tier 1 ASes are at the top of this hierarchy, consisting of large backbone providers that peer with one another without paying transit fees. These networks have access to the entire global routing table without purchasing IP transit from any other provider. Below them are Tier 2 ASes, which may peer with other networks but also purchase transit to access parts of the Internet not reachable through peering alone. Finally, Tier 3 ASes typically rely entirely on upstream providers for Internet connectivity and are often regional ISPs or enterprise networks.

The relationships between autonomous systems are defined by agreements such as peering or transit contracts. Peering relationships allow two ASes to exchange traffic directly, often without monetary exchange, benefiting both parties by reducing transit costs and improving performance. Transit relationships, on the other hand, involve one AS paying another for the ability to send traffic to the broader Internet. These relationships are negotiated between networks and enforced using BGP policies, giving rise to the rich and intricate web of connections that define the Internet's topology.

One of the most critical aspects of autonomous systems is their role in influencing the path that data takes from source to destination. When a data packet traverses the Internet, it often passes through multiple ASes before reaching its endpoint. Each AS along the path evaluates available routes and makes decisions based on its policies, commercial agreements, and technical considerations. The path a packet takes may not always be the shortest in terms of physical distance, but it will reflect the routing preferences and agreements of the ASes involved.

The interactions between ASes also have significant implications for Internet resilience and redundancy. Since each AS operates independently, the failure of a single network does not necessarily disrupt global connectivity. BGP allows ASes to advertise multiple routes to the same destination, so if one AS experiences an outage or a link fails, traffic can be rerouted through alternative paths. This decentralized design contributes to the Internet's remarkable ability to recover from disruptions, whether they are caused by hardware failures, natural disasters, or intentional attacks.

Despite this robustness, the autonomy of ASes also introduces challenges. Misconfigurations, such as accidental route leaks or incorrect prefix announcements, can have widespread impacts due to the interconnected nature of the Internet. A single AS announcing incorrect routing information can cause traffic misdirection, service outages, or even facilitate malicious activities like BGP hijacking. This reality underscores the importance of proper routing policies, filtering mechanisms, and security measures to ensure the stability and security of the Internet's routing infrastructure.

Autonomous systems continue to evolve in response to technological advancements and changing business models. The rise of content delivery networks, cloud service providers, and large-scale data centers has shifted traffic patterns and increased the prominence of certain ASes. Additionally, the growing trend of network automation and software-defined networking is influencing how ASes manage and optimize routing. Yet, despite these changes, the core principles behind autonomous systems—independence, control, and policy-driven routing—remain as relevant today as they were at the dawn of the modern Internet.

Understanding autonomous systems is key to appreciating how the Internet functions at both a technical and economic level. These networks, each operating according to its own rules yet interconnected through BGP, collectively enable the global exchange of data that powers everything from simple web browsing to mission-critical financial transactions. The dynamic interactions between ASes shape the Internet's performance, resilience, and accessibility, making them a foundational concept in the world of networking.

The Evolution from EGP to BGP

The transition from the Exterior Gateway Protocol (EGP) to the Border Gateway Protocol (BGP) marked one of the most significant milestones in the history of Internet routing. This shift not only transformed the technical landscape of inter-network communication but also enabled the Internet to scale from a limited research network to the massive, decentralized, and commercialized system we depend on today. Understanding this evolution provides critical insight into the foundational principles that shaped the architecture and resilience of the modern Internet.

In the early days of the Internet, during the late 1970s and early 1980s, the network was relatively small and centralized. The Advanced Research Projects Agency Network (ARPANET), the precursor to today's Internet, connected a modest number of academic and research institutions. As this network began expanding, it became necessary to develop a method for routing data between different, independently operated networks. The Exterior Gateway Protocol, formalized in 1982 with RFC 904, was introduced to facilitate communication between autonomous systems, which were networks under distinct administrative control.

EGP served the Internet well in its formative years, but it was inherently designed for a hierarchical topology. It relied on a tree-like structure in which routing information flowed from a single core network outward to connected networks. This design worked adequately when the Internet resembled a hub-and-spoke model, with a central backbone network providing the main conduit for traffic.

However, as the Internet grew and new autonomous systems emerged, the limitations of EGP became apparent. Networks were no longer just passive recipients of connectivity; they sought to establish direct peering relationships with each other, bypassing the centralized core to improve performance and reduce costs.

The rigidity of EGP's hierarchical model prevented it from supporting the peer-to-peer relationships that were now in demand. EGP lacked the flexibility to manage more complex topologies where multiple autonomous systems interconnected dynamically. Furthermore, EGP's routing decisions were simplistic, based solely on reachability rather than more granular policies or path selection criteria. These shortcomings created operational inefficiencies and made it clear that a new protocol was required to meet the evolving needs of the growing Internet community.

By the late 1980s, the need for a more robust and scalable inter-domain routing protocol led to the creation of BGP. The protocol was designed by Yakov Rekhter and Kirk Lougheed, whose goal was to develop a solution that would accommodate the emerging reality of a decentralized Internet. BGP introduced a completely different approach to routing compared to its predecessor. Instead of enforcing a strict hierarchy, BGP allowed autonomous systems to operate as peers, freely exchanging routing information and making independent policy decisions.

The first version of BGP was documented in RFC 1105 in 1989. Unlike EGP, BGP operated as a path vector protocol. It introduced the AS_PATH attribute, a crucial feature that recorded the sequence of autonomous systems a route traversed. This simple yet powerful mechanism enabled BGP to prevent routing loops, a problem that EGP could only address through its rigid tree structure. BGP's path vector model allowed for a more accurate and flexible representation of the Internet's increasingly meshed topology.

As the Internet transitioned from a government-funded research network to a global, commercially driven infrastructure in the early 1990s, the adoption of BGP accelerated. The decommissioning of the National Science Foundation Network (NSFNET) backbone in 1995 was a pivotal event that reinforced the need for a decentralized routing system. Private backbone providers took on the responsibility of global transit, and BGP facilitated the complex peering relationships and routing policies that enabled this distributed model to function efficiently.

BGP's policy-based routing capabilities allowed autonomous systems to define routing decisions based on factors beyond mere reachability. Networks could prioritize routes based on business agreements, performance considerations, or security concerns. This level of control empowered network operators to shape traffic flows according to their specific needs, fostering a competitive and adaptable Internet ecosystem. The flexibility to influence inbound and outbound traffic became a critical advantage, especially for large service providers and enterprises with multi-homed network architectures.

Another critical development that solidified BGP's role in the Internet's evolution was the introduction of Classless Inter-Domain Routing (CIDR) in the mid-1990s. CIDR, which BGP-4 fully supported, addressed the issue of IPv4 address exhaustion by allowing more efficient aggregation of IP prefixes. This innovation significantly reduced the size of global routing tables, alleviating the strain on router memory and processing power as the number of networks and routes continued to grow.

Despite its numerous advantages, the transition from EGP to BGP was not without challenges. The flexibility of BGP introduced complexities in routing policy management and troubleshooting. Furthermore, the decentralized nature of BGP exposed new vulnerabilities, such as route leaks and BGP hijacking, which have persisted as security concerns to this day. Nonetheless, the benefits of BGP's autonomy, scalability, and adaptability far outweighed the limitations of EGP's rigid structure.

As BGP matured, it became the backbone protocol supporting not just the public Internet but also private networks, VPNs, and MPLS infrastructures. Its extensibility allowed for the addition of new features and capabilities, ensuring its relevance in emerging technologies such as IPv6 adoption, cloud computing, and software-defined networking. Unlike EGP, which was ultimately constrained by its design philosophy, BGP has continuously evolved alongside the

Internet, adapting to meet the demands of an ever-changing landscape.

The evolution from EGP to BGP was more than a technical upgrade; it represented a paradigm shift in how networks interconnect and collaborate globally. By moving away from centralized control toward distributed autonomy, BGP laid the groundwork for the open, resilient, and interconnected Internet that supports billions of users, devices, and services worldwide. The freedom for networks to negotiate their own peering and transit relationships while maintaining global interoperability is a testament to BGP's enduring design principles. The protocol's success and longevity are reflected in its continued use today, decades after its introduction, as the critical routing mechanism that keeps the Internet running.

BGP Versions: From 1 to 4

The Border Gateway Protocol, commonly referred to as BGP, has evolved significantly since its inception, adapting to the Internet's rapid expansion and increasing complexity. The history of BGP versions reflects both technological innovation and the need to address the operational realities of a global, decentralized network. From BGP-1 to BGP-4, each iteration introduced critical enhancements to scalability, functionality, and resilience. Examining the development of these versions provides valuable insight into how BGP became the backbone of modern inter-domain routing.

BGP-1, the first version of the protocol, was introduced in 1989 and documented in RFC 1105. It emerged at a time when the Internet was transitioning from a small research network into a more commercial and decentralized system. BGP-1 was created to replace the aging and inflexible Exterior Gateway Protocol (EGP), which could no longer support the increasing complexity of the Internet's topology. One of the core innovations of BGP-1 was the introduction of the path vector model. This model allowed for greater autonomy and flexibility among autonomous systems (ASes), which could now independently determine how to route traffic based on their own policies. BGP-1 featured the AS_PATH attribute, which tracked the autonomous systems that a route traversed, helping to prevent routing loops and allowing for more informed path selection.

Although BGP-1 laid the foundation for inter-domain routing, it was still experimental. It was deployed in a limited number of networks, primarily to address immediate issues stemming from the growing interconnectedness of the early Internet. Its success, however, revealed areas where additional refinement was necessary, particularly in terms of stability and scalability. These limitations paved the way for the next version of the protocol.

BGP-2 followed shortly after, arriving in 1990 and documented in RFC 1163. This version incorporated lessons learned from early BGP-1 deployments and made improvements in areas such as message formatting and state machine stability. While BGP-2 did not introduce groundbreaking new features, it provided a more mature and reliable framework for routing between autonomous systems. BGP-2 clarified key aspects of the protocol, helping operators implement and manage BGP sessions more effectively. The introduction of incremental updates—allowing BGP routers to send only changes rather than the full routing table—marked a significant improvement in efficiency, reducing both processing load and bandwidth consumption.

Even as BGP-2 became operational, it was clear that further enhancements would be required to accommodate the Internet's ongoing expansion. In response, BGP-3 was introduced in 1991 and documented in RFC 1267. This version represented a significant evolution, bringing BGP closer to the fully-featured and robust protocol that the Internet required. BGP-3 refined the protocol's state machine, enhancing session stability and improving the handling of connection failures between BGP peers. It also made further improvements to the protocol's ability to handle large routing tables and introduced additional attributes that enriched the policy control mechanisms available to network operators.

At this stage, the Internet was growing rapidly, driven by the rise of commercial Internet service providers and the increasing demand for public access to global networks. BGP-3 served as a critical stepping stone in this process, supporting the Internet's shift from a primarily academic and government-run network to a commercial infrastructure capable of supporting businesses and private users. Despite these improvements, the introduction of Classless Inter-Domain Routing (CIDR) was still on the horizon, and the need to address the exhaustion of IPv4 address space loomed large.

In response to these challenges, BGP-4 was introduced in 1995, documented in RFC 1771 and later superseded by RFC 4271, which remains the authoritative specification today. BGP-4 was a landmark release that solidified BGP's role as the standard protocol for inter-domain routing. One of the most important innovations in BGP-4 was its full support for CIDR. CIDR allowed for the aggregation of IP address prefixes, significantly reducing the size of global routing tables and mitigating the pace of IPv4 address exhaustion. This change alone made BGP-4 indispensable for the rapidly expanding Internet.

BGP-4 also introduced other enhancements that strengthened the protocol's scalability and flexibility. The addition of route aggregation capabilities enabled autonomous systems to advertise summarized routes, simplifying routing tables across the Internet and improving efficiency. BGP-4 expanded the range of routing policies that network operators could implement by offering greater control over attributes such as LOCAL_PREF and MULTI_EXIT_DISC (MED). These attributes gave operators more granular control over both inbound and outbound traffic flows, allowing them to optimize routing based on business agreements, performance goals, or security considerations.

In addition to these features, BGP-4 laid the groundwork for future extensibility through the introduction of optional transitive attributes. This modular approach made it possible to extend the protocol with additional features without breaking backward compatibility. Over the years, this design decision has allowed BGP-4 to evolve alongside emerging technologies and requirements, including support for Multi-Protocol BGP (MP-BGP) to enable routing for multiple network layer protocols such as IPv6, VPNv4, and VPNv6.

BGP-4 also benefited from improvements to its stability and robustness. The introduction of mechanisms such as route flap dampening and support for route refresh reduced the likelihood of instability caused by frequent route changes. These features contributed to the protocol's ability to handle the increasingly dynamic nature of the Internet, where routing adjustments are made frequently due to changes in topology, traffic demands, and network outages.

Today, BGP-4 remains the backbone of Internet routing, supporting billions of devices and thousands of autonomous systems. Its longevity is a testament to the careful design choices and continuous evolution that have allowed it to remain relevant through decades of technological change. While the basic principles established in BGP-1 persist—such as the path vector model and policy-driven routing—the enhancements made in each subsequent version, culminating in BGP-4, have enabled the Internet to grow far beyond what its creators originally envisioned.

As the Internet continues to evolve, with trends such as automation, SDN, and cloud-native architectures becoming more prevalent, BGP-4 remains an essential component of global network infrastructure. Its ability to adapt and extend through new drafts, standards, and vendor-specific enhancements ensures that BGP will continue to play a central role in the operation and development of the Internet. The story of BGP's progression from version 1 to version 4 is a reflection of the Internet's own evolution—from a modest research project to the vast, resilient, and decentralized system that supports modern life across the globe.

How BGP Works at a High Level

At its core, the Border Gateway Protocol (BGP) is a routing protocol that allows autonomous systems, or ASes, to exchange routing information and make policy-driven decisions on how to route traffic across the global Internet. Operating at the application layer, BGP is fundamentally different from interior gateway protocols like OSPF or IS-IS, which focus on routing within a single organization or network. BGP, instead, is designed to connect disparate networks, each with its own policies and priorities, into a cohesive system that enables end-to-end communication across the Internet. Understanding how BGP works at a high level involves exploring how routers establish connections, exchange routing information, and make decisions based on a combination of technical metrics and business-driven policies.

BGP routers, commonly referred to as BGP speakers, communicate with each other through a session established over the Transmission Control Protocol (TCP), typically on port 179. This use of TCP ensures reliable delivery of messages, providing a level of stability and order essential for maintaining routing information. A BGP session, or peering relationship, is established between two routers when both agree to exchange routing information. These peers can be located within the same autonomous system, which is known as internal BGP (iBGP), or across different autonomous systems, known as external BGP (eBGP). Regardless of whether the session is internal or external, the fundamental mechanics of the protocol remain the same.

Once a BGP session is established, the routers begin exchanging routing information, referred to as BGP updates. These updates contain information about IP prefixes that the router knows how to reach, as well as a set of attributes associated with each prefix. Unlike traditional distance-vector protocols, which may rely solely on hop count or cost metrics, BGP's path vector model leverages a collection of attributes to inform routing decisions. The most basic and essential attribute is the AS_PATH, which lists all the autonomous systems a route has traversed. This allows routers to avoid routing loops, as a router can easily detect if its own AS number appears in the path and discard the route if necessary.

In addition to AS_PATH, BGP updates can carry several other attributes, such as NEXT_HOP, LOCAL_PREF, MULTI_EXIT_DISC (MED), and various community tags. The NEXT_HOP attribute specifies the IP address of the next router along the path to the destination network, while LOCAL_PREF is used within an AS to influence outbound traffic decisions. MED provides a mechanism for influencing inbound routing decisions when there are multiple links between two autonomous systems. Community tags, which are optional and transitive, provide operators with the ability to group routes and apply routing policies in bulk.

Once a BGP router receives updates from its peers, it does not automatically forward all received routes to other peers. Instead, it processes the received information using a sophisticated decision-making process to select the best path for each destination. This process follows a series of rules defined by the protocol, often referred to as the BGP decision process. The router evaluates multiple routes based on various criteria, including the highest LOCAL_PREF, the shortest AS_PATH, the lowest origin type, the lowest MED, and other factors such as the router ID or the lowest IP address of the BGP peer if tie-breaking is needed.

After selecting the best path for each destination, the router installs these routes into its routing information base (RIB), which is a table that stores all routing information collected from BGP peers. From there, the best routes are injected into the forwarding information base (FIB) or the main routing table of the router, where they can be used to forward actual traffic. Only after this selection process are the chosen routes propagated to other BGP peers, ensuring that each router shares its most preferred path with its neighbors.

BGP is fundamentally policy-driven, meaning that routing decisions are not based purely on technical metrics but also on business policies defined by network administrators. Each autonomous system can apply filters and manipulate attributes to enforce policies that reflect contractual agreements, security concerns, or traffic engineering objectives. For example, an AS may choose to prefer one upstream provider over another due to lower costs, or it may restrict the advertisement of certain prefixes to select peers for security reasons.

One of the defining characteristics of BGP is that it operates in a decentralized manner. There is no single controlling authority dictating how traffic flows globally. Instead, each AS independently decides how to handle routing based on the information received from peers and its internal policies. This decentralized structure is what gives the Internet its resilience, redundancy, and flexibility. When a network link fails or an AS experiences an outage, BGP can react by withdrawing routes associated with the affected paths and recalculating alternate paths through other autonomous systems. This dynamic nature enables the Internet to self-heal and maintain connectivity in the face of disruptions.

BGP's operation extends beyond traditional IPv4 routing. With the introduction of Multi-Protocol BGP (MP-BGP), BGP gained the capability to carry routing information for multiple network protocols, including IPv6, VPNs, and MPLS labels. This versatility has allowed

BGP to serve as the routing foundation not only for the global public Internet but also for private enterprise networks and service provider backbones. MP-BGP allows network operators to manage diverse routing requirements under a unified protocol, streamlining operations and reducing complexity.

Another key element of BGP's high-level operation is its scalability. The Internet comprises tens of thousands of autonomous systems and millions of IP prefixes. BGP handles this immense scale through its efficient incremental update mechanism, which minimizes the amount of routing information exchanged after the initial session establishment. Instead of constantly sending full routing tables, BGP routers only send changes, reducing bandwidth consumption and improving convergence times.

Despite its strengths, BGP is not without challenges. The protocol assumes that participating autonomous systems are well-behaved and trustworthy. However, misconfigurations or malicious activity, such as prefix hijacking, can lead to incorrect routing information propagating across the Internet, causing service disruptions or enabling traffic interception. To mitigate these risks, techniques such as prefix filtering, route validation, and Resource Public Key Infrastructure (RPKI) have been introduced, adding security layers to protect the integrity of BGP routing information.

At a high level, BGP functions as the glue holding together the complex network of autonomous systems that form the global Internet. Its ability to convey routing information between independently operated networks while allowing each to enforce its own policies has enabled the Internet to grow and adapt to ever-changing demands. From supporting simple routing decisions to enabling sophisticated traffic engineering and multi-protocol routing, BGP continues to serve as a cornerstone of global interconnectivity. Its high-level operation is a delicate balance of technical precision and policy control, providing the framework that ensures data can travel efficiently and reliably across the world.

The BGP Finite State Machine

The Border Gateway Protocol (BGP) is built upon a well-defined structure that governs how routers establish and maintain sessions with their peers. Central to this structure is the BGP Finite State Machine (FSM), a crucial component that ensures reliability, order, and predictability in BGP's operation. The BGP FSM describes the series of states through which a BGP session progresses, from its initial attempt to connect to a peer, all the way to a fully established and active session where routing information is exchanged. Understanding the BGP FSM provides insight into how routers manage peer relationships, detect failures, and recover from disruptions, forming the backbone of stable inter-domain routing across the Internet.

The BGP FSM is a state-driven model with six distinct states: Idle, Connect, Active, OpenSent, OpenConfirm, and Established. Each state represents a specific phase in the lifecycle of a BGP session. When a BGP speaker attempts to initiate or maintain a peering session with another router, it moves through these states sequentially based on specific triggers and events. This design allows BGP to handle connection attempts methodically and recover gracefully from network failures or configuration errors.

The Idle state is the starting point for every BGP session. In this state, the BGP speaker is not actively trying to establish a connection. Instead, it is waiting for administrative instructions to initiate or accept a session. In practical terms, a router in the Idle state may be waiting for the operator to configure a new peer or for network conditions to meet predefined policies before attempting to form a session. If configured to initiate a connection, the router will proceed to the Connect state.

In the Connect state, the BGP speaker attempts to establish a TCP connection to the remote peer. Since BGP operates over TCP, the stability and reliability of this underlying transport protocol are critical. If the TCP connection is successfully established, the FSM progresses to the OpenSent state. However, if the TCP attempt fails due to issues like peer unreachability or network congestion, the router will transition to the Active state, where it will continue to retry connection attempts periodically. In the Connect state, the FSM may also revert to Idle if administrative policies or timers dictate a reset.

The Active state reflects a situation where the router is actively attempting to connect but has not yet succeeded. This could result from transient network problems, such as a peer being temporarily down or intermediate links being unavailable. BGP is designed to be persistent, and the router will continue to retry the connection at regular intervals as defined by its internal timers. If a TCP connection is eventually established during this phase, the FSM transitions forward to OpenSent. If not, the router may return to Idle before cycling back to Active, repeating the attempt based on its backoff strategy.

The OpenSent state is reached once the TCP session is established, and the BGP speaker has sent an Open message to its peer. This message includes critical information such as the ASN, BGP version, hold time, and BGP identifier. The speaker now awaits an Open message from the remote peer. If the peer responds with a valid Open message and the parameters are acceptable to both parties, the FSM proceeds to the OpenConfirm state. However, if the peer responds with an error or a mismatch in critical values such as ASN or BGP version, the router will terminate the session and transition back to Idle. Security policies, such as authentication mismatches, may also trigger a reset at this stage.

Upon reaching the OpenConfirm state, both routers have successfully exchanged Open messages and must now confirm the liveliness of the session through the exchange of Keepalive messages. These lightweight messages function as a heartbeat, ensuring that the session remains active and both routers are responsive. If the Keepalive exchange is successful, the FSM moves into the Established state, where the core functionality of BGP begins.

The Established state represents a fully operational BGP session where routing information is exchanged. In this state, routers can send and receive BGP Update messages, advertising routes and associated attributes to their peers. BGP can also send Notification messages if an error occurs, terminating the session if necessary. Once in the Established state, routers continuously exchange Keepalives to maintain the session. If the TCP session fails or a fatal error occurs, the session will drop, and the FSM will return to the Idle or Active state, depending on the nature of the failure.

The BGP FSM is not only a technical formality but also a key aspect of the protocol's fault tolerance. By cycling through states such as Active and Connect, BGP can withstand intermittent network failures without collapsing entirely. The design also enforces a disciplined approach to session management, preventing routers from repeatedly flooding peers with connection requests and reducing unnecessary load on the network.

Each transition between states in the FSM is governed by specific events, including successful TCP handshakes, the reception of valid or invalid Open messages, timer expirations, and administrative resets. Timers, such as the ConnectRetry timer, play an essential role in pacing these transitions to avoid overwhelming network resources. Additionally, the FSM's structure provides valuable diagnostic information to network engineers. By observing which state a BGP session is in, operators can quickly identify issues such as peer misconfigurations, TCP-level problems, or incompatibilities between routers.

The FSM also plays a crucial role in security and stability. For example, if a router receives an unexpected or malformed message during any phase, it can immediately terminate the session and revert to Idle, helping to protect against certain types of attacks or misconfigurations. Similarly, the FSM ensures that routing updates only occur in the Established state, preventing incomplete or unauthorized sessions from influencing routing tables.

In the broader context of the Internet, where thousands of autonomous systems form peering relationships through BGP, the FSM guarantees a standardized and predictable method for establishing and maintaining those sessions. Every router that participates in BGP, whether in a small enterprise network or a global Tier 1 provider, follows this state machine, ensuring interoperability and consistency across diverse platforms and network environments.

The simplicity and reliability of the BGP FSM have contributed to BGP's longevity and success. While extensions to BGP, such as Multi-Protocol BGP or BGP Graceful Restart, have introduced new capabilities, the fundamental operation of the FSM has remained largely unchanged. This stability has allowed network engineers to rely on familiar behavior when designing and troubleshooting BGP deployments.

By guiding routers through a deliberate process of connection attempts, message exchanges, and session validation, the BGP Finite State Machine serves as a safeguard for the protocol's critical role in routing the world's Internet traffic. It embodies the discipline and rigor required to sustain a system where every peering relationship has the potential to impact the global Internet's performance and reliability.

Peering Agreements and Relationships

The Internet's decentralized architecture is built on the concept of independent networks, known as autonomous systems, connecting and exchanging traffic with one another. These interconnections are formalized through peering agreements and relationships, which form the economic and technical foundation of global Internet routing. Unlike a centrally managed system, the Internet relies on a web of negotiated partnerships between networks, where each autonomous system determines how and with whom it shares routing information and traffic. Peering is at the core of this decentralized system and plays a critical role in shaping how data flows across continents, countries, and regions.

Peering refers to the direct interconnection between two autonomous systems for the purpose of exchanging traffic. This exchange is facilitated through Border Gateway Protocol (BGP) sessions, where each party advertises its IP prefixes to the other. While BGP is the protocol that enables routing between these networks, the terms under which the networks agree to exchange traffic are governed by peering agreements. These agreements can be formalized through written contracts or established as informal, handshake-style arrangements based on mutual benefit. Regardless of their formality, peering relationships are fundamental to how the Internet operates on a daily basis.

The motivation behind peering is largely economic and operational. Networks peer with one another to reduce transit costs, improve network performance, and exert greater control over traffic flows. By peering directly, networks can exchange traffic without having to pay a third-party transit provider, which can significantly lower operational expenses. This cost savings is particularly attractive to Internet service providers (ISPs), content delivery networks (CDNs), and large enterprises that move substantial volumes of data. In addition to lowering costs, peering relationships can enhance performance by reducing the number of hops between source and destination networks, thereby lowering latency and improving the user experience.

Peering relationships typically fall into two broad categories: public peering and private peering. Public peering occurs at Internet Exchange Points (IXPs), which are shared physical infrastructures where multiple networks colocate and interconnect. At an IXP, a network can establish BGP sessions with many potential peers over a single physical port, leveraging a shared switching fabric. This model provides an efficient way to peer with multiple networks in one location, reducing the need for numerous individual connections. IXPs are especially popular in major metropolitan areas and serve as critical hubs for regional and international Internet traffic.

Private peering, on the other hand, involves the establishment of a dedicated physical connection between two networks, usually in a data center or colocation facility. Private peering is preferred when the volume of exchanged traffic between two networks is sufficiently high to justify the cost of dedicated infrastructure. This model provides greater control over the peering relationship, allows for fine-tuned traffic engineering, and eliminates the potential for congestion associated with shared environments like IXPs.

The decision to peer is not solely driven by traffic volumes or technical considerations; it is also influenced by the business interests and policies of the autonomous systems involved. Networks generally follow one of three main business models in establishing relationships: settlement-free peering, paid peering, and transit. Settlement-free peering, also known as bilateral or reciprocal peering, involves the exchange of traffic without monetary compensation. This model is common when two networks exchange roughly equal amounts of traffic or when the peering arrangement benefits both parties equally in terms of cost savings or performance improvements.

Paid peering occurs when one network compensates another for the privilege of direct interconnection. This model may be used when one party perceives a disproportionate benefit or when the balance of traffic between networks is significantly asymmetric. For instance, a smaller regional ISP might pay a larger content provider for direct access to their network to improve customer experience. In contrast, transit relationships involve one network paying another for full access to the global Internet via the provider's upstream connections. Transit is different from peering in that it is a customer-provider relationship rather than a partnership of equals.

Peering policies are another layer of complexity in the formation of relationships. Each autonomous system defines its own peering criteria, which may include minimum traffic thresholds, geographic presence, network performance standards, or business requirements. Some networks maintain open peering policies, welcoming connections from any willing party at shared facilities like IXPs. Others maintain restrictive or selective peering policies, choosing to peer only with networks that meet specific technical or economic conditions. These policies are often published in routing registries or on the network's website, providing transparency to potential peers.

The dynamics of peering relationships are influenced by the evolving nature of Internet traffic patterns. The rise of content-heavy services such as video streaming, cloud computing, and large-scale content delivery networks has shifted traffic flows, placing increased importance on peering relationships between content providers and access networks. In some cases, disputes over peering terms have resulted in well-publicized de-peering events, where networks temporarily sever their BGP sessions, leading to degraded connectivity or slower performance for end-users. These disputes highlight the business-driven nature of peering and the delicate balance between cooperation and competition among network operators.

The technical implementation of peering is largely standardized through BGP, but the operational practices surrounding it can vary widely. Networks may implement route filtering to ensure that only authorized prefixes are exchanged, preventing the spread of incorrect or malicious routing information. Communities and BGP attributes are often used to tag and control the propagation of routes, providing networks with tools to enforce their traffic engineering strategies and business policies.

Peering agreements also contribute to the resilience and redundancy of the global Internet. By establishing multiple peering relationships with diverse networks, autonomous systems create alternate paths for traffic, ensuring that outages or performance degradation in one path do not result in complete service disruptions. This diversity of paths contributes to the Internet's ability to reroute traffic dynamically and withstand localized failures, enhancing the overall reliability of the network.

The landscape of peering continues to evolve alongside technological and business developments. The growing adoption of automation and software-defined networking is streamlining peering operations, enabling networks to establish and manage peering relationships more dynamically. Additionally, emerging protocols and practices, such as the use of RPKI for route origin validation, are improving the security and trustworthiness of routing information exchanged between peers.

Ultimately, peering agreements and relationships form the fabric of global interconnectivity. They shape how data flows across networks, impact the cost structures of Internet service providers, and influence the end-user experience on a daily basis. Behind every BGP session lies a series of business negotiations, technical considerations, and strategic decisions, all contributing to the complex and collaborative nature of the Internet.

Internal vs. External BGP

The Border Gateway Protocol, or BGP, serves as the backbone of inter-domain routing on the Internet, providing the mechanism by which autonomous systems exchange routing information. Within the framework of BGP, there are two distinct operational modes: Internal BGP (iBGP) and External BGP (eBGP). While both variants utilize the same underlying protocol and message types, they are used in fundamentally different contexts and are governed by different operational rules. Understanding the contrast between iBGP and eBGP is essential to comprehending how networks maintain both internal consistency and external connectivity.

External BGP, or eBGP, is used to exchange routing information between different autonomous systems. This is the form of BGP most commonly associated with the Internet's decentralized structure. When two autonomous systems decide to interconnect, either through peering agreements or transit relationships, their respective routers establish eBGP sessions. These eBGP peers then exchange network reachability information, advertising which IP prefixes are accessible through their networks. The AS_PATH attribute, which records the sequence of autonomous systems a route has traversed, is particularly relevant in eBGP. With each hop between autonomous systems, an AS number is appended to the AS_PATH. This provides a clear record of the path taken by a route, enabling downstream routers to make informed decisions based on path length and origin.

The standard configuration for eBGP peers is that they are typically connected on directly adjacent routers, often via a dedicated point-to-point link or a shared Internet Exchange Point (IXP). This adjacency is significant because, in eBGP, the default behavior is to consider routes received from an external peer as eligible for redistribution to other peers within the local AS or to other external peers. This design reflects the typical role of eBGP in distributing information across administrative boundaries, where one AS is informing its neighbors of routes it can reach or transit.

In contrast, Internal BGP, or iBGP, is used within a single autonomous system. It enables routers within the same AS to share routing information learned from external sources. For example, if a network has multiple eBGP connections to different upstream providers, iBGP allows that externally learned information to propagate throughout the internal routers of the AS, ensuring that all routers have a consistent view of the available external paths. One of the key operational rules of iBGP is the iBGP split-horizon rule, which states that routes learned via iBGP must not be advertised to other iBGP peers. This rule is designed to prevent routing loops within the AS, but it introduces the need for a full mesh of iBGP sessions among all BGP routers within the AS.

The full-mesh requirement for iBGP means that every iBGP-speaking router must establish a direct session with every other iBGP router in the network. While feasible in small networks, this requirement becomes burdensome as the number of routers grows, since the number of sessions increases quadratically. To address this scalability challenge, network operators often deploy route reflectors or BGP confederations. Route reflectors act as focal points within the AS, receiving routes from iBGP peers and reflecting them to other iBGP peers, thereby reducing the total number of required sessions. Confederations, on the other hand, allow an AS to be divided into smaller sub-ASes that exchange routes internally as if they were separate autonomous systems, but appear as a single AS to external networks.

Another key distinction between eBGP and iBGP lies in route attributes and their treatment. eBGP typically has a shorter AS_PATH since it reflects inter-AS hops, while iBGP routes maintain the AS number unchanged, as all routers belong to the same autonomous system. In addition, attributes like LOCAL_PREF and MED are often leveraged in iBGP to influence routing decisions within the AS. LOCAL_PREF, for instance, is an attribute used internally to dictate the preferred path for outbound traffic. A higher LOCAL_PREF value will generally cause a route to be preferred over others. This attribute is not exchanged with external peers via eBGP but is critical in iBGP for managing intra-AS routing policies.

While eBGP is more outward-facing, handling relationships with external networks, iBGP is focused on disseminating and maintaining consistency of routing information inside the AS. In many cases, large service providers and enterprises operate both eBGP and iBGP simultaneously. Routers on the edge of the network will run eBGP to connect with external peers, such as upstream providers or other networks, and then redistribute that information internally using iBGP. This allows for a clear demarcation between external routes and internal routing policies.

The way BGP next-hop addresses are handled also differs between the two variants. In eBGP, when a router advertises a route to an external peer, it modifies the NEXT_HOP attribute to its own IP address. In iBGP, however, the NEXT_HOP attribute is preserved. This means that iBGP routers must ensure that the next-hop IP is reachable within the IGP (Interior Gateway Protocol) domain, as the next-hop might still reference an external address learned via eBGP.

Additionally, administrative distance, a value used by routers to select the most preferred route when multiple protocols offer the same destination, distinguishes eBGP and iBGP. Most router platforms assign eBGP a lower administrative distance (commonly 20) compared to iBGP (commonly 200), making eBGP-learned routes preferable when competing with iBGP-learned routes for the same destination.

Both iBGP and eBGP play complementary roles in building a network's routing framework. eBGP is crucial for enabling external connectivity and defining how an autonomous system participates in the global Internet. It allows network operators to implement routing policies based on business relationships, such as peering and transit agreements, and to engineer traffic for optimal performance and cost efficiency. On the other hand, iBGP provides the mechanism for internal distribution of routing information learned from eBGP peers, ensuring that routers within the AS have the necessary knowledge to forward traffic to external destinations.

Together, iBGP and eBGP form the core structure through which networks control both external and internal routing behaviors. Their interactions influence how traffic flows between organizations and how resilience is maintained in the face of outages or link failures. The distinction between these two operational modes also shapes how networks are architected, from simple single-homed setups to highly redundant and geographically distributed infrastructures.

In large-scale networks, the thoughtful deployment of iBGP and eBGP is essential for achieving operational efficiency, policy enforcement, and network stability. Whether balancing traffic across multiple upstream providers or optimizing the flow of data within a sprawling backbone, network engineers must leverage the distinct characteristics of both iBGP and eBGP to build networks that are both efficient and resilient. The success of the Internet as a distributed system is rooted in this duality, where external relationships and internal consistency are managed by two sides of the same protocol.

BGP Route Selection Process

The Border Gateway Protocol is designed to provide networks with the ability to exchange routing information across autonomous systems and make independent decisions about how data is routed to specific destinations. At the heart of BGP's functionality is its route selection process, a critical mechanism that determines which path a router will choose when multiple routes to the same destination are available. This process is highly structured, following a well-defined sequence of criteria to ensure consistency, predictability, and alignment with the routing policies of each network. Unlike some protocols that make routing decisions based purely on metrics like hop count or link cost, BGP evaluates a series of attributes that reflect both technical considerations and administrative policies.

When a BGP router receives multiple advertisements for the same IP prefix from different peers, it must choose a single best route to install in its routing table and advertise to its own neighbors. The router does not forward all available paths, but instead selects one based on a hierarchical decision-making process. This decision process is deterministic and applies the same rules every time a selection must be made, ensuring consistent behavior across routers and networks.

The first and most important criterion in the BGP route selection process is the weight attribute, which is a Cisco-specific, non-transitive attribute used locally within a router. The weight is the first decision factor because it is not shared between routers and provides administrators with the ability to influence routing on a specific device. A route with a higher weight is always preferred over one with a lower weight, regardless of other attributes. Since weight is locally significant, it does not affect how other routers select routes but can play a key role in controlling outbound traffic within a particular router.

If the weight is equal for all competing routes, BGP next considers the LOCAL_PREF attribute. LOCAL_PREF, or local preference, is used within an autonomous system to influence how routers choose outbound paths. Unlike weight, LOCAL_PREF is shared between routers inside the same AS and is used to signal a preferred exit point for traffic. A route with a higher LOCAL_PREF is preferred over one with a lower value. This attribute is commonly used by network administrators to direct traffic through specific upstream providers or preferred links, especially in multi-homed environments.

If LOCAL_PREF values are also equal, BGP proceeds to examine the route's origin attribute. The origin indicates how a route was introduced into BGP and can have one of three values: IGP (indicating the route was learned from an Interior Gateway Protocol), EGP (from the legacy Exterior Gateway Protocol), or INCOMPLETE (typically learned through redistribution from other routing protocols). BGP prefers routes with an IGP origin over EGP, and EGP over INCOMPLETE. While this attribute holds less sway in modern networks, it is still part of the decision hierarchy.

The next step involves comparing the AS_PATH length. BGP prefers routes with a shorter AS_PATH, as this indicates fewer autonomous systems to traverse. A shorter path is generally interpreted as a more direct route, potentially reducing latency and the number of possible points of failure. However, it is essential to recognize that while AS_PATH length is a critical factor, it can be deliberately manipulated through techniques such as AS_PATH prepending, where an AS artificially lengthens its path to make it less preferred by other networks.

If AS_PATH lengths are identical, BGP evaluates the MULTI_EXIT_DISC attribute, often abbreviated as MED. The MED is used to convey a preferred entry point into an AS when multiple links exist between two neighboring autonomous systems. A lower MED value is preferred over a higher one. MED is an optional, non-transitive attribute, meaning that it is shared only between directly connected ASes and is not propagated beyond them. It is particularly useful in scenarios where one AS wants to influence inbound routing decisions made by its neighboring AS.

If the MED values are also equal, BGP gives preference to external BGP (eBGP) routes over internal BGP (iBGP) routes. This rule aligns with the general expectation that an eBGP-learned route likely represents a more authoritative or direct path to a destination compared to one learned internally through iBGP. This criterion helps maintain the consistency and policy alignment of the BGP decision process within autonomous systems.

If the tie still persists, BGP selects the route with the lowest IGP metric to the BGP NEXT_HOP. This step reflects the router's internal topology. The IGP metric evaluates how close the NEXT_HOP address is within the local network, preferring the route whose next-hop IP address is reachable with the lowest cost or fewest internal hops. This criterion ensures that traffic exits the AS using the most efficient internal path to the external peer.

Should the IGP metrics also tie, BGP compares router IDs. The router ID is a unique identifier, typically the highest IP address assigned to a loopback interface or the highest active IP address on the router. The route from the peer with the lowest router ID is preferred. If the router IDs are also the same, which is highly unlikely in practice but possible in misconfigured networks, BGP finally falls back to selecting the route from the peer with the lowest BGP neighbor IP address.

This deterministic, step-by-step route selection process ensures that BGP routers make routing decisions in a uniform and predictable way. Each criterion is applied in order until a single best route emerges from the set of available paths. While this process appears linear and straightforward, network operators frequently manipulate BGP attributes to influence routing decisions intentionally. By adjusting LOCAL_PREF values, prepending AS_PATHs, or setting MEDs, operators can engineer traffic flows to meet specific business or performance objectives.

BGP's route selection process is also deeply intertwined with the autonomy of each network. Since every autonomous system defines its own routing policies, two networks may select different paths for the same destination based on their unique business relationships, technical requirements, or cost structures. This independence allows for flexibility and competition in the global Internet, but it also means

40

that routing outcomes may not always align with purely technical metrics such as shortest path or lowest latency.

The process also highlights BGP's role as a policy-driven protocol. Unlike purely distance-based or link-cost-based routing protocols, BGP allows operators to make routing decisions that incorporate non-technical factors, such as financial agreements or regulatory compliance. This policy-rich framework has enabled BGP to serve as the routing protocol of choice for complex, multi-provider environments and for the broader Internet, where economic and contractual considerations are as important as technical efficiency.

Ultimately, the BGP route selection process underpins the stability and resilience of the Internet's routing system. By providing a structured method for evaluating competing routes and selecting a single best path, BGP ensures that data can flow consistently and reliably across diverse and independently operated networks. The balance between automation and operator control in this process has made BGP a uniquely adaptable and powerful tool in modern networking.

BGP Attributes Explained

The Border Gateway Protocol is unique among routing protocols due to its policy-driven nature, and at the center of this capability are its attributes. BGP attributes are pieces of information attached to route advertisements that guide routers in the selection, propagation, and filtering of routes. These attributes empower network operators to implement granular control over routing behavior, both within an autonomous system and across external interconnections with other networks. Understanding BGP attributes is essential to fully appreciating how BGP operates, as these elements influence the decisions BGP routers make every time multiple paths to the same destination exist.

BGP attributes are broadly categorized into four types: well-known mandatory, well-known discretionary, optional transitive, and optional non-transitive. These categories indicate how attributes are treated by BGP-speaking routers, whether they are required, whether they must be propagated to other routers, and how they impact interoperability across different networks. Well-known attributes are universally recognized and supported by all BGP implementations, ensuring a consistent baseline for route selection and propagation. Optional attributes, on the other hand, offer additional flexibility and can be leveraged for specific use cases or enhanced routing policies.

The AS_PATH attribute is one of the most critical well-known mandatory attributes. It provides a record of the sequence of autonomous systems a route advertisement has passed through before reaching a given router. Each time a route crosses an autonomous system boundary via an external BGP session, the AS number of the upstream AS is prepended to the AS_PATH. This attribute plays a dual role. First, it helps prevent routing loops, as a router will reject any route that already contains its own AS number in the AS_PATH. Second, it provides valuable information to influence routing decisions, as shorter AS_PATHs are generally preferred by BGP routers, based on the assumption that fewer autonomous system hops equate to a more direct and efficient path.

Another crucial well-known mandatory attribute is the NEXT_HOP. This attribute specifies the IP address of the next-hop router to which packets should be forwarded to reach the advertised destination network. In eBGP, the NEXT_HOP is typically the IP address of the peer router that sent the update. In iBGP, the NEXT_HOP attribute is preserved, meaning that the next-hop IP may point to an eBGP neighbor, requiring internal routers to ensure the next-hop is reachable via the internal routing protocol, such as OSPF or IS-IS. The NEXT_HOP attribute plays a vital role in the BGP route selection process, especially when routers evaluate the IGP cost to reach the next-hop during the decision-making process.

The LOCAL_PREF attribute is a well-known discretionary attribute used exclusively within an autonomous system to influence outbound routing decisions. LOCAL_PREF indicates the degree of preference for a route within an AS, with higher values being favored over lower ones. This attribute allows network operators to dictate preferred exit points when multiple eBGP peers offer paths to the same destination. For instance, an operator may assign a higher LOCAL_PREF to a route learned from a provider offering better pricing or lower latency, ensuring that internal routers prioritize that path. Since LOCAL_PREF is propagated to all iBGP routers within the AS but is not shared with external peers, it is a powerful tool for shaping internal routing policies.

The ORIGIN attribute is another well-known mandatory attribute that identifies the origin of the route and how it was introduced into BGP. There are three possible values: IGP, EGP, and INCOMPLETE. A route with an IGP origin is considered to have been injected into BGP from an Interior Gateway Protocol like OSPF or IS-IS, while EGP refers to the legacy Exterior Gateway Protocol, which BGP replaced. INCOMPLETE is used when a route is redistributed into BGP from a source other than an IGP or EGP, such as from static or directly connected routes. Although modern networks rarely rely on this attribute for routing decisions, it remains part of the BGP decision-making process.

The MULTI_EXIT_DISC attribute, commonly abbreviated as MED, is an optional non-transitive attribute that helps influence how external neighbors choose inbound paths when multiple entry points exist between two autonomous systems. A lower MED value is preferred over a higher one. Since MED is non-transitive, it is not propagated beyond the neighboring AS. MED is especially useful when an AS wishes to indicate a preferred ingress point for specific traffic flows, without enforcing hard policies on the remote AS. For example, a multi-homed AS may advertise different MED values on separate eBGP sessions to suggest optimal points for inbound traffic.

BGP communities are an example of optional transitive attributes, providing a versatile tagging mechanism that allows network operators to group and apply policies to multiple routes collectively. A community is a 32-bit value, often expressed in the format of two 16-bit numbers separated by a colon, such as 65000:100. Communities are powerful because they allow operators to influence the behavior of other routers within or even outside their autonomous system. For example, a transit provider may offer its customers the ability to tag routes with specific communities to control how traffic is treated, such as limiting propagation to certain peers or adjusting LOCAL_PREF on the provider's network. Extended communities, a variation of standard BGP communities, expand this functionality by increasing the available tag space and supporting more granular policies.

Another key attribute, often associated with traffic engineering, is the atomic aggregate attribute, a well-known discretionary attribute that signals route summarization. When a router aggregates several smaller prefixes into a larger one, the atomic aggregate attribute indicates that some of the original, more specific route information may have been lost. This is relevant in networks where route summarization is used to reduce the size of routing tables and simplify advertisements to peers, though the aggregated prefix may represent multiple subnets internally.

Additionally, the aggregator attribute, an optional transitive attribute, complements the atomic aggregate attribute by identifying the router and AS that performed the aggregation. This attribute is primarily informational but can help network operators trace the source of summarized prefixes, which can be useful for troubleshooting or auditing routing behaviors.

The flexibility provided by BGP attributes is one of the protocol's defining strengths. Network operators have the ability to manipulate these attributes through route maps, policies, and filters to implement highly customized routing behaviors. For instance, by adjusting LOCAL_PREF internally and AS_PATH prepending externally, an AS can influence both how its outbound and inbound traffic flows through its network and how remote networks perceive the attractiveness of its routes.

Ultimately, BGP attributes are the building blocks that allow autonomous systems to assert control over routing decisions, enforce business agreements, and optimize network performance. They enable BGP to transcend simple distance-based metrics and provide a policy-rich environment where each network's unique requirements and strategies are reflected in the paths chosen for data to traverse. Mastery of BGP attributes is essential for engineers tasked with designing, operating, and securing the infrastructure that underpins global Internet connectivity.

The Role of AS_PATH

Among the many attributes that define the behavior of the Border Gateway Protocol, the AS_PATH attribute stands out as one of the most critical components for both routing decisions and overall Internet stability. The AS_PATH plays a dual role: it prevents routing loops and serves as a key metric in the BGP route selection process. Every autonomous system that participates in BGP relies on AS_PATH to understand how a route has traversed the global network and to determine whether that route is acceptable or preferable compared to others. The simplicity and effectiveness of AS_PATH have made it a cornerstone of BGP's design since the protocol's earliest versions.

At its core, the AS_PATH attribute is a sequential list of autonomous system numbers that a particular route has passed through. Each time a BGP route crosses an autonomous system boundary via an external BGP session, the router at that boundary appends its own AS number to the beginning of the AS_PATH list. This process creates a historical record of the path a route has taken through the Internet, making it possible for routers further downstream to evaluate the route based on its journey. If a route originated in AS 100, passed through AS 200, and then through AS 300 before reaching AS 400, the AS_PATH would be recorded as 100 200 300 when advertised to AS 400.

The most fundamental role of AS_PATH is loop prevention. BGP is a path vector protocol, and one of the core design goals is to ensure that routing loops, which can cause instability and inefficiency, are avoided. Each BGP router examines the AS_PATH of incoming route advertisements to determine whether its own AS number is present. If it detects its own AS number in the AS_PATH, the route is rejected immediately. This check ensures that no route will be accepted that would send traffic back into the same AS it came from, thus eliminating the possibility of a loop occurring across autonomous system boundaries.

Beyond its function as a safeguard against loops, AS_PATH also plays a major role in route selection. When multiple routes to the same destination prefix are available, BGP favors the route with the shortest AS_PATH length. The reasoning is straightforward: a shorter AS_PATH generally represents a more direct route through fewer autonomous systems, which is often interpreted as a more efficient or desirable path. Although this metric is not always a perfect reflection of real-world network performance—since AS boundaries do not directly correlate to physical distances or link capacities—it remains one of the most influential factors in BGP's decision-making process.

In practice, the AS_PATH can be deliberately manipulated through a technique known as AS_PATH prepending. In this approach, a network artificially lengthens the AS_PATH of routes it advertises by adding its own AS number multiple times at the beginning of the path. For example, instead of advertising a route as having come directly from AS 65001, a network might prepend its AS number two or three times, making the AS_PATH appear as 65001 65001 65001. This tactic makes the route less attractive to neighboring autonomous systems because it appears longer and, therefore, less preferable. AS_PATH prepending is commonly used for traffic engineering purposes, allowing networks to influence inbound traffic by signaling to external peers that certain paths should be considered less favorable, without relying on the cooperation of external networks.

The AS_PATH also serves as a valuable diagnostic tool for network operators and engineers. By examining the AS_PATH associated with a specific route, operators can gain insight into the path that traffic will take across the Internet, identify unexpected or suboptimal routing patterns, and troubleshoot network performance issues. For example, if a network administrator notices that traffic destined for a nearby region is being routed through distant autonomous systems, an inspection of the AS_PATH can reveal where and why this divergence occurs. The AS_PATH provides transparency into the flow of data and the relationships between autonomous systems, making it indispensable for effective network management.

Another important aspect of the AS_PATH is its use in implementing routing policies. Many networks apply filters to inbound and outbound BGP updates based on the AS_PATH. A provider might, for instance, block prefixes originating from certain AS numbers to prevent blackhole routes, hijacks, or undesirable traffic patterns. Similarly, an ISP may prefer routes learned through specific partners by deprioritizing routes containing AS numbers associated with less favorable peering agreements. By crafting policies around AS_PATH attributes, networks can exert considerable control over their routing behavior and ensure alignment with both technical objectives and business agreements.

It is also worth noting that the AS_PATH reflects the structure of the Internet's autonomous system topology. The Internet is composed of thousands of autonomous systems, ranging from large Tier 1 providers to regional ISPs and enterprise networks. The AS_PATH offers a lens into this interconnected web, illustrating how data must often traverse multiple independent networks to reach its final destination. While the path length is one factor in this equation, the specific ASes listed in the AS_PATH can reveal peering relationships, transit dependencies, and even geopolitical routing dynamics.

Security considerations have also elevated the significance of the AS_PATH attribute in recent years. Incidents involving route leaks or BGP hijacking often involve manipulation or spoofing of AS_PATH data. To combat these threats, mechanisms like Resource Public Key Infrastructure (RPKI) and BGPsec have been introduced to improve the validation and cryptographic security of routing information. RPKI helps verify that the originating AS in the AS_PATH is authorized to announce a given prefix, while BGPsec seeks to provide cryptographic protection for the entire AS_PATH, ensuring that each step in the path is verifiable and authentic.

In the context of multi-homed networks, which connect to multiple upstream providers, the AS_PATH is also a tool for balancing traffic. A network may choose to advertise shorter AS_PATHs to preferred providers while prepending AS numbers on advertisements to other providers, influencing how remote networks select return paths for inbound traffic. This level of control is particularly useful for optimizing performance, balancing bandwidth usage, or aligning with contractual obligations between providers.

The AS_PATH is not just a technical artifact of BGP but a critical component that reflects the distributed nature of the Internet. Its ability to enforce loop prevention, influence routing decisions, support traffic engineering, and offer operational transparency underscores its centrality to inter-domain routing. Every BGP router on the Internet consults the AS_PATH when determining how to route traffic, making it a vital part of the system that keeps global connectivity intact. From the simplest stub network to the largest international backbone provider, the AS_PATH attribute remains one of the most relied-upon mechanisms for maintaining order and efficiency in Internet routing.

The Power of LOCAL_PREF

Within the Border Gateway Protocol, the LOCAL_PREF attribute holds a unique and influential position. Unlike attributes such as AS_PATH, which are used to influence decisions based on external factors between autonomous systems, LOCAL_PREF is purely an internal tool that networks use to control their outbound routing decisions. It is a well-known discretionary BGP attribute, meaning that while it is not mandatory, it is widely recognized and implemented across all BGP-capable routers. The power of LOCAL_PREF lies in its ability to dictate policy within a single autonomous system, offering engineers fine-grained control over how traffic exits the network. This internal focus is what makes LOCAL_PREF indispensable for service providers, enterprises, and content delivery networks managing multiple upstream providers or peering points.

When a BGP router receives multiple routes to the same destination prefix, it must determine which one is the most preferred. The LOCAL_PREF attribute is one of the first factors evaluated during the BGP route selection process. In fact, LOCAL_PREF is considered even before external factors like AS_PATH length or MED values are taken into account. A route with a higher LOCAL_PREF value will always be preferred over routes with lower values, regardless of the path length or origin type. This positioning early in the decision-making process gives LOCAL_PREF a significant impact on how traffic flows out of an autonomous system.

LOCAL_PREF is particularly useful in multi-homed environments where a network has multiple connections to upstream providers or peers. By manipulating LOCAL_PREF values, network operators can influence which egress point a particular destination prefix will use. For example, if a network is connected to two upstream providers—Provider A and Provider B—administrators may set a higher

LOCAL_PREF for routes received from Provider A. As a result, all routers within the autonomous system will prefer to send traffic to destinations reachable via Provider A, effectively steering outbound traffic according to the organization's preferences. This might be done because Provider A offers lower latency, more favorable business terms, or better reliability compared to Provider B.

What makes LOCAL_PREF so versatile is its ability to enforce a consistent policy across the entire autonomous system. Unlike attributes such as weight, which is locally significant and only applies to a single router, LOCAL_PREF is propagated through internal BGP sessions to all routers within the AS. This ensures that all routers share the same routing perspective, resulting in coordinated decision-making. In large networks, this consistency is crucial for preventing routing asymmetries or traffic blackholing caused by conflicting preferences on different routers.

Another powerful aspect of LOCAL_PREF is its role in traffic engineering. Network operators can assign LOCAL_PREF values based on more granular criteria, such as specific IP prefixes, groups of prefixes, or even classes of traffic. For instance, critical application traffic destined for business partners might be routed through the most stable and highest-performance provider by assigning those prefixes a higher LOCAL_PREF, while less critical or bulk traffic could be sent through a lower-cost provider with a lower LOCAL_PREF. This level of control enables organizations to implement policies that balance cost, performance, and redundancy based on business needs.

In addition to influencing routing decisions based on business objectives, LOCAL_PREF can also be used in conjunction with dynamic conditions. Network operators may integrate LOCAL_PREF manipulation into automated systems that respond to real-time network telemetry. For example, if a specific provider experiences a degradation in performance or an outage, automation systems could temporarily reduce the LOCAL_PREF associated with routes received from that provider. This would cause traffic to be rerouted through alternate providers, helping maintain service quality during periods of instability. When normal service resumes, the LOCAL_PREF values can be restored automatically, minimizing operational overhead and improving network resilience.

Another common use case for LOCAL_PREF is during maintenance events. When an operator plans to perform maintenance on one of its outbound links or upstream providers, it can reduce the LOCAL_PREF values of routes learned via that provider prior to taking the link offline. This action ensures that traffic naturally shifts to alternative providers without requiring manual intervention on every router or risking sudden traffic loss during the maintenance window. LOCAL_PREF's influence at the AS-wide level simplifies such operations and helps maintain seamless service continuity for end-users.

In service provider environments, LOCAL_PREF is often integrated into customer-specific policies. For example, large ISPs might offer customers premium routing services where certain customers pay for routes to be preferred over others. In this scenario, the provider may assign higher LOCAL_PREF values to routes advertised by or for premium customers, ensuring that their outbound traffic takes the shortest or most desirable egress paths. This approach provides providers with a tool for differentiating services and aligning technical configurations with customer service level agreements (SLAs).

The implementation of LOCAL_PREF is typically done through route maps, policy statements, or prefix lists combined with routing policies. These tools allow network administrators to apply LOCAL_PREF settings in a highly controlled manner. Route maps, for instance, can match on specific route attributes, such as the source of the route, specific prefixes, BGP communities, or other criteria, and then set or modify the LOCAL_PREF accordingly. This mechanism provides a modular and scalable way to apply routing policies across a network, especially in large and complex environments where hundreds or thousands of routes must be managed simultaneously.

It is important to note that while LOCAL_PREF is effective at controlling outbound traffic, it does not directly influence inbound traffic from external networks. Inbound traffic engineering typically requires cooperation from neighboring autonomous systems or the use of other BGP attributes like AS_PATH prepending or selective prefix advertisements. However, by shaping how traffic exits the network, LOCAL_PREF indirectly impacts how the AS utilizes its external connectivity and balances usage among its peers and providers.

From a troubleshooting and operational perspective, LOCAL_PREF is one of the first attributes network engineers examine when investigating unexpected routing behavior. If traffic is taking an unintended egress point or if route preferences seem inconsistent with policy objectives, checking LOCAL_PREF values is often the first step. Misconfigured or conflicting LOCAL_PREF settings can lead to suboptimal routing or even traffic imbalances that strain certain providers while underutilizing others.

Ultimately, the power of LOCAL_PREF lies in its simplicity and effectiveness. It grants network operators clear and authoritative control over outbound traffic flows, providing a crucial mechanism for aligning routing behavior with both business and technical objectives. In the complex and dynamic world of Internet routing, where autonomous systems must constantly balance cost, performance, and reliability, LOCAL_PREF remains an essential tool that supports informed and flexible decision-making across diverse network infrastructures.

MED and Inter-AS Path Selection

The MULTI_EXIT_DISC attribute, commonly known as MED, plays a subtle yet important role in the Border Gateway Protocol, particularly when it comes to influencing how autonomous systems select ingress points when multiple paths exist between two neighboring networks. MED is an optional, non-transitive attribute used primarily in inter-AS path selection, offering a mechanism for one autonomous system to signal its routing preference to an adjacent AS. While MED does not carry the same broad influence as attributes like LOCAL_PREF or AS_PATH, it is a valuable tool for influencing routing behavior on the edge of networks and can have significant operational impact in multi-homed or heavily interconnected environments.

MED is designed to solve a specific problem that arises when two autonomous systems, say AS 100 and AS 200, have multiple interconnection points between them. Without a mechanism like MED, AS 200 would have no way of knowing which entry point AS 100 prefers for traffic destined to its prefixes. While LOCAL_PREF allows an AS to control outbound traffic within its own network, MED allows an AS to suggest inbound traffic preferences to a neighboring AS. By attaching a MED value to its route advertisements, AS 100 can indicate which link or path it would prefer AS 200 to use when sending traffic. The lower the MED value, the more preferred the route is to the receiving autonomous system. This mechanism provides a way to achieve rudimentary inbound traffic engineering, although it relies on the cooperation and configuration of the neighboring AS to be effective.

One of the defining characteristics of MED is that it is non-transitive. This means that the MED attribute is not propagated beyond the neighboring AS. If AS 100 sends a MED value to AS 200, AS 200 will not pass that MED value to AS 300 or any other downstream networks. This localized scope reflects MED's intended purpose as a bilateral signal used to manage preferences between directly connected networks. It is not designed to influence global routing decisions across multiple autonomous systems but to provide neighboring ASes with insight into the advertising AS's ingress point preferences.

The deployment of MED is common in scenarios where multiple interconnection points exist between two networks, such as between a large ISP and a regional ISP or between two Tier 2 providers. For example, consider AS 100 with presence in both New York and Chicago, connected to AS 200 in both cities. AS 100 may prefer inbound traffic from AS 200 to enter via its New York interconnection for specific prefixes and through Chicago for others, depending on factors such as network topology, cost structures, or performance objectives. By setting a lower MED on advertisements in New York for certain prefixes, AS 100 can suggest that AS 200 prefer that interconnection point for those routes.

While MED provides a valuable tool for inter-AS traffic management, its influence is not absolute. MED is only considered after several other BGP attributes in the route selection process. It is evaluated after LOCAL_PREF, AS_PATH length, and origin type. Therefore, a higher LOCAL_PREF value or a shorter AS_PATH will typically override the MED value. This ordering ensures that internal routing policies and broader inter-domain routing considerations take precedence over the more localized preferences signaled by MED.

In many networks, MED is only honored under specific conditions. Some autonomous systems will compare MED values only when routes are received from the same neighboring AS. This means that MED values from different ASes are often ignored to prevent conflicting preferences from influencing route selection globally. However, some networks may choose to enable global MED comparison, evaluating MED values even when received from different autonomous systems, but this is less common due to the potential for inconsistent routing behavior.

Another aspect of MED is its use in conjunction with other traffic engineering techniques. While MED influences the ingress path into an AS, it is often combined with AS_PATH prepending or selective prefix advertisements to create more sophisticated routing strategies. For example, a network might prepend its AS_PATH on certain routes to make them less attractive globally while simultaneously setting a low MED on a preferred interconnection point to manage traffic from a specific peer. This layered approach allows for greater control over both inbound and outbound traffic flows.

Despite its utility, MED can also introduce complexity into routing operations. Since it relies on the neighboring AS to honor and implement the preference, inconsistent configurations or conflicting policies can lead to unexpected results. For instance, if AS 200 applies its own LOCAL_PREF or disregards MED entirely, the traffic flow may not align with the intentions of AS 100. Additionally, if the MED values are set incorrectly or fail to account for network conditions, they can inadvertently cause suboptimal routing decisions, such as sending traffic over congested or less-preferred links.

MED is also subject to the effects of route aggregation. When routes are aggregated by a router, the individual MED values of the more specific routes may be lost, as only a single MED value can be attached to the resulting summary route. This behavior can complicate traffic engineering efforts, especially in large networks where route summarization is employed to reduce routing table size. To mitigate this, some networks choose to limit the use of aggregation on prefixes that require precise inbound traffic control via MED.

In addition to technical considerations, MED is influenced by business and operational dynamics between peers. Networks with symmetrical relationships, such as settlement-free peering arrangements, are often more likely to honor each other's MED preferences, as both parties have an interest in maintaining balanced and efficient traffic flows. However, in customer-provider relationships, providers may prioritize their own policies or revenue optimization strategies over a customer's MED preferences, particularly if traffic volume imbalances or capacity constraints exist.

To further enhance the utility of MED, some networks use community strings in combination with route maps to dynamically set MED values based on specific routing policies. For example, an AS may use communities to categorize routes by service type, geographic location, or customer class, applying different MED values depending on these factors. This dynamic approach enables more granular control and the ability to adjust preferences quickly in response to changing network conditions or business requirements.

Ultimately, MED serves as a key mechanism for influencing inter-AS path selection when multiple connections exist between the same two networks. It provides a valuable means of guiding inbound traffic into an AS and aligns with the broader goals of traffic engineering and routing policy enforcement. Although it operates within a narrower scope compared to attributes like LOCAL_PREF or AS_PATH, the strategic application of MED can significantly enhance network performance, resilience, and cost management, particularly for networks with complex peering and transit relationships. Understanding and leveraging MED effectively allows network operators to shape traffic flows in a way that optimizes the operational and business interests of their autonomous system.

BGP Next Hop Attribute

The NEXT_HOP attribute is one of the most essential elements within the Border Gateway Protocol, as it directly informs routers of where to forward packets to reach a particular destination prefix. Every route advertisement in BGP includes a NEXT_HOP attribute, which specifies the IP address of the next-hop router along the path to the advertised destination. While other attributes like AS_PATH or LOCAL_PREF influence the decision-making process behind route selection, the NEXT_HOP attribute provides the critical information needed to actually forward packets at the data plane level. Without it, routers would lack the necessary instructions to complete the journey of a packet beyond their own network.

At a fundamental level, the NEXT_HOP attribute serves to identify the next router that must be used to reach the destination network. For external BGP (eBGP) sessions, where routers from different autonomous systems exchange routing information, the NEXT_HOP is usually set to the IP address of the eBGP peer that originated the advertisement. This means that when Router A in AS 100 receives a route advertisement from Router B in AS 200, the NEXT_HOP for that route will be the IP address of Router B. This information enables Router A to correctly forward any traffic destined for that advertised prefix to Router B, trusting that Router B will then forward it to its next destination.

Within internal BGP (iBGP) sessions, the behavior of the NEXT_HOP attribute differs. When a router receives a route from an eBGP peer and advertises that route internally to other iBGP peers, it does not modify the NEXT_HOP attribute. This means that the next-hop IP remains as the external IP address of the original eBGP peer. For example, if Router A receives a prefix from Router B and advertises it to Router C via iBGP, Router C will see the NEXT_HOP as Router B's IP address, not Router A's. This behavior requires that all routers within an autonomous system be able to reach the external IP address of Router B, which is often located at the AS boundary. Therefore, interior routing protocols like OSPF or IS-IS must ensure that next-hop reachability is preserved within the autonomous system.

This distinction between eBGP and iBGP next-hop behavior serves a purpose. In eBGP, the router modifies the NEXT_HOP because the two peers are typically directly connected, and each autonomous system is expected to control its own forwarding. In iBGP, however, the preservation of the NEXT_HOP allows internal routers to have visibility into the actual external point of entry into the AS, enabling more intelligent routing decisions based on where the external peer resides in the network topology.

In certain topologies, particularly those involving multiple border routers or route reflectors, the NEXT_HOP attribute can present operational challenges. Since iBGP does not automatically update the NEXT_HOP, internal routers might learn about a prefix but be unable to forward traffic toward the next-hop if the external peer's IP is unreachable. This is where the concept of next-hop-self comes into play. By configuring the next-hop-self command on a BGP session, an iBGP-speaking router will rewrite the NEXT_HOP to its own IP address before advertising the route to internal peers. This ensures that downstream routers can always forward packets toward an accessible and reachable router within the AS, resolving potential reachability issues.

The importance of the NEXT_HOP attribute extends beyond simple forwarding. It is also a key input in the BGP route selection process. If multiple routes are available for the same destination prefix and all higher-priority attributes, such as LOCAL_PREF and AS_PATH, result in a tie, BGP will prefer the route with the lowest IGP metric to reach the NEXT_HOP. In this context, the IGP metric refers to the internal routing cost calculated by protocols like OSPF or IS-IS to reach the IP address indicated by the NEXT_HOP attribute. By factoring in the internal routing cost, BGP ensures that the most efficient internal path is selected when determining which egress point to use for outbound traffic.

The NEXT_HOP attribute also plays a significant role in multi-protocol BGP (MP-BGP) environments, where routes for other protocols, such as VPNv4 or IPv6, are advertised. In these cases, the NEXT_HOP may be set to a loopback interface or a provider edge (PE) router within a VPN, and it can even carry information for labeled paths in MPLS networks. For instance, when dealing with MPLS Layer 3 VPNs, the NEXT_HOP attribute in BGP advertisements will carry the IP address of the ingress PE router. This value is critical for correct MPLS label imposition and transport within the provider's core network.

In addition to technical implications, the NEXT_HOP attribute can also impact traffic engineering strategies. For example, in large networks with multiple external connections and geographically diverse border routers, network operators can influence which exit point internal routers use by adjusting IGP metrics toward the NEXT_HOP addresses. Lowering the IGP cost to one border router's IP over another can guide routers to prefer one external egress point over another, without modifying BGP attributes like LOCAL_PREF or MED. This approach provides flexibility by allowing internal IGP adjustments to affect outbound routing decisions while leaving BGP policies intact.

When analyzing BGP operations in complex networks, the NEXT_HOP attribute is frequently a focal point in troubleshooting. If internal routers cannot reach the NEXT_HOP IP of a learned route due to IGP issues, incomplete route redistribution, or incorrect filtering, traffic may be blackholed or suboptimally routed. Verifying next-hop reachability is often one of the first troubleshooting steps network engineers perform when diagnosing route propagation or traffic forwarding anomalies within an autonomous system.

Security considerations around the NEXT_HOP attribute also emerge in multi-tenant environments or networks with shared infrastructure. Ensuring that NEXT_HOP information is not inadvertently leaked between customers or into unauthorized areas of the network is critical to preventing unauthorized traffic redirection or denial of service. Route maps, prefix lists, and next-hop filtering mechanisms are employed to mitigate such risks and to ensure routing integrity across administrative boundaries.

As networks evolve to support automation and software-defined networking, the role of the NEXT_HOP attribute remains fundamental. In automated environments, dynamic control of IGP metrics or next-hop manipulation through configuration management systems allows operators to adjust routing behavior rapidly in response to network changes, failures, or business-driven routing policies.

Ultimately, the NEXT_HOP attribute is indispensable in bridging BGP's control plane decisions with the actual forwarding of packets at the data plane level. It is the critical piece of information that connects the logical concept of route selection with the physical or logical pathways that packets must traverse to reach their destinations. In every BGP network, from small enterprise environments to global service provider backbones, the NEXT_HOP attribute functions quietly yet decisively, ensuring that traffic is forwarded efficiently, securely, and according to the policies defined by network operators. Its role underscores the importance of seamless integration between BGP and underlying IGPs, highlighting how foundational concepts like next-hop reachability continue to shape the flow of traffic across the modern Internet.

The Importance of BGP Communities

BGP communities are one of the most versatile and powerful tools available to network engineers for controlling and influencing routing policies within and across autonomous systems. Introduced as an optional transitive attribute, communities allow network operators to attach additional metadata to BGP route advertisements. This metadata provides contextual information or instructions that can be used to apply routing policies automatically, reducing manual intervention and streamlining operations. While communities are not directly involved in the BGP decision process itself, their presence enables precise control over how routes are propagated, filtered, preferred, or even suppressed, both internally and when shared with external peers.

The basic structure of a BGP community is a 32-bit value, typically represented in the format of two 16-bit numbers separated by a colon, such as 65000:100. The first part of the community value is often the autonomous system number of the network defining the community, while the second part is a numeric code representing a specific routing instruction or category. For instance, a service provider might define 65000:200 to indicate that a route should be advertised only to certain peers or to signal that specific policies should be applied downstream.

One of the most common uses of BGP communities is in traffic engineering. Networks use them to influence how their prefixes are treated once they leave their own autonomous system. For example, a customer network connected to a service provider might tag its routes with communities that instruct the provider to set particular LOCAL_PREF values on those routes, affecting how outbound traffic from the provider's network is routed. Alternatively, the customer might use communities to request AS_PATH prepending on specific upstream links to de-preference certain paths for inbound traffic. This ability to influence upstream behavior without requiring direct configuration access to external routers is one of the key benefits of BGP communities.

BGP communities are also used extensively for controlling route propagation. A network can tag routes with communities that instruct its peers or transit providers to limit where those routes are advertised. For example, a community might signal that a route should be shared with peer networks but not with upstream transit providers, thereby controlling the spread of prefixes and preventing unnecessary or undesired global visibility. This selective advertisement capability helps improve routing efficiency and ensures that prefixes are only advertised where needed, reducing the size of global routing tables and avoiding unintended routing paths.

Another critical use case for BGP communities is the implementation of blackholing for DDoS mitigation. Many service providers offer customers the ability to signal blackhole requests by tagging routes with specific community values. When a prefix is advertised with a blackhole community, the provider will often discard traffic destined for that prefix at its network edge, preventing malicious traffic from reaching the customer's infrastructure. This approach allows customers to quickly respond to volumetric attacks and mitigate their impact without needing to coordinate complex manual interventions during an active incident.

Communities also play an essential role in simplifying policy management across large and complex networks. In scenarios where a network has dozens or even hundreds of peers and customers, communities allow for the centralization of routing logic. Instead of applying individual route-maps or filters for every routing decision, network operators can use communities to group and classify routes, applying consistent policies across multiple peers or links automatically. For example, all customer routes tagged with a community such as 65000:300 might be assigned a specific LOCAL_PREF or might be restricted to certain interconnection points within a provider's backbone.

Extended communities further expand this concept by offering a larger address space and additional subtypes to support more advanced policies, especially in MPLS VPN environments. Extended communities can carry more information, such as route targets and route distinguishers, which are critical components in building Layer 3 VPNs and ensuring customer route isolation. These extensions make BGP communities not only a tool for policy control but also a fundamental building block for services like VPNs, inter-provider VPN peering, and other advanced multi-tenant architectures.

Despite their technical power, BGP communities are also heavily influenced by business relationships and agreements between networks. Service providers often define well-known community values that their customers can use to leverage specific services or behaviors. These documented community values are typically shared via network peering documents or public Internet Routing Registries (IRRs). For instance, a provider may publish a list of communities that customers can use to request lower LOCAL_PREF on certain routes, influence route suppression in certain regions, or control advertisements to specific Internet exchange points. These predefined policies enhance transparency and give customers the autonomy to manage their own traffic engineering needs within the framework established by the provider.

The importance of BGP communities also becomes evident in Internet Exchange Points (IXPs), where multiple networks interconnect. IXPs frequently standardize on community-based tagging to control which peers receive specific routes. A member of an IXP may tag its prefixes with communities that limit advertisements to a subset of peers based on geography, traffic type, or business agreements. This type of control improves peering efficiency, prevents accidental route leaks, and allows networks to better tailor their interconnection strategies.

Another reason why BGP communities are essential is their ability to automate otherwise complex routing policies in dynamic environments. In modern networks where traffic patterns can shift rapidly due to cloud service deployments, content distribution, or regional traffic surges, the ability to automatically apply routing policies based on community tags saves significant time and reduces the risk of manual configuration errors. Automation systems and orchestration tools often rely on community tagging as a mechanism to implement large-scale policy changes programmatically, aligning with trends in network automation and software-defined networking.

Network operators must also consider security implications when implementing community-based routing policies. In the absence of strict input filtering, malicious actors or misconfigured customers could inadvertently apply communities that result in unintended routing behaviors. To mitigate this, networks often deploy inbound community filtering on customer and peer sessions, ensuring that only authorized community values are accepted and processed. This safeguards routing integrity and prevents unauthorized manipulation of routing policies.

BGP communities ultimately provide a level of abstraction that decouples routing policy from static, per-peer configurations. They allow for scalable, flexible, and context-aware routing control, enabling networks to respond to technical, operational, and business demands with agility. From traffic engineering and DDoS mitigation to route visibility control and VPN service delivery, communities are integral to modern BGP deployments. Their significance lies not only in their technical function but also in their role as a communication mechanism between autonomous systems, facilitating cooperation and alignment in a complex and competitive global Internet environment. The widespread adoption and continued evolution of BGP communities highlight their enduring value in shaping how networks interact, optimize, and secure the exchange of routing information.

BGP Confederations

As the Internet expanded and networks grew in size and complexity, scalability challenges with the Border Gateway Protocol became increasingly apparent. One of the most significant scalability issues within BGP is the requirement for a full mesh of internal BGP sessions between all routers in a single autonomous system. In other words, in a traditional iBGP environment, every router running iBGP must establish a direct BGP session with every other iBGP-speaking router within the same autonomous system. While this requirement is manageable for small or moderately sized networks, it becomes impractical in large networks where hundreds of routers are deployed. The resulting number of sessions grows exponentially, leading to increased CPU utilization, memory consumption, and management overhead. To address this problem, BGP confederations were introduced as one of the methods to improve scalability while preserving the integrity and functionality of BGP's routing architecture.

A BGP confederation allows a single autonomous system to be divided into multiple smaller, sub-autonomous systems, each identified by a unique sub-AS number. These sub-ASes are grouped under a larger, overarching AS, known as the confederation identifier. From the outside world, the entire confederation is viewed as a single AS, using the confederation identifier as the global AS number in BGP updates sent to external autonomous systems. However, within the confederation, the internal sub-AS numbers are visible and used to reduce the number of iBGP sessions required between routers.

The introduction of sub-AS boundaries inside the larger autonomous system allows network operators to establish eBGP sessions between routers in different sub-ASes within the confederation. These internal eBGP sessions behave similarly to traditional eBGP sessions, including the resetting of the BGP Time to Live (TTL) value, the sending of the AS_PATH attribute, and the modification of NEXT_HOP attributes. However, because these sub-AS numbers are stripped out and replaced by the confederation identifier when routes are advertised to external autonomous systems, the Internet at large remains unaware of the internal confederation structure.

One of the key benefits of confederations is their ability to reduce the full-mesh requirement within each sub-AS. Inside a sub-AS, routers are still required to establish a full mesh of iBGP sessions, but the number of routers within a sub-AS is significantly smaller compared to the entire network. Between sub-ASes, operators can leverage eBGP-like sessions, which do not require a full mesh, and instead, routes can propagate via hierarchical or more scalable designs. This segmentation helps improve control over routing policy and minimizes overhead related to route reflection or full-mesh management across massive topologies.

Confederations are often compared to route reflectors, another popular solution to address iBGP scalability issues. While route reflectors also reduce the number of iBGP sessions required by allowing routers to reflect routes to other iBGP peers, they can sometimes introduce complexity related to route reflection clusters, redundant paths, or non-optimal routing decisions due to the "hot potato" effect. Confederations, in contrast, mimic natural AS boundaries and offer more predictable policy enforcement points between sub-ASes. However, it is not uncommon for large service providers and enterprises to deploy both route reflectors and confederations together, creating a hybrid solution tailored to their specific network topology and operational needs.

Beyond scalability, BGP confederations also offer policy flexibility. Since the routers between sub-ASes communicate using eBGP-like sessions, network operators can apply more granular routing policies between different parts of the network. For instance, different sub-ASes may represent geographically distinct regions or different service domains within a large organization. By treating inter-sub-AS routing similarly to external routing, operators can implement prefix filtering, LOCAL_PREF adjustments, MED manipulation, and other eBGP policy mechanisms to influence how traffic flows within the confederation. This flexibility is particularly useful for service providers who need to apply different policies between network regions, manage traffic engineering objectives, or enforce security segmentation.

However, the use of confederations introduces additional considerations related to AS_PATH manipulation. Because sub-AS numbers are included in the AS_PATH attribute inside the confederation, it becomes possible to apply policies based on sub-AS-specific path selection. This internal visibility aids in troubleshooting and operational management, allowing engineers to trace routing behavior through different sub-AS boundaries. Yet, once routes leave the confederation, these sub-AS numbers are removed from the AS_PATH and replaced by the confederation identifier, ensuring that external networks see a single contiguous AS.

Confederations also help networks achieve better administrative autonomy and decentralization. In large organizations or service providers, network teams responsible for different regions or business units can operate sub-ASes with a degree of independence, defining local routing policies while still conforming to broader, confederation-wide routing policies. This modular approach supports network growth and simplifies operational management by breaking down large-scale networks into more manageable components.

From a routing perspective, the BGP decision process treats routes learned from confederation peers slightly differently than traditional eBGP peers. Specifically, when a router receives a route from a confederation peer, it considers it as if it were an iBGP-learned route when determining whether to re-advertise that route to other iBGP peers within the same sub-AS. This prevents routing loops and ensures that the split-horizon rule applied to iBGP sessions is still respected within sub-AS boundaries. This nuance further highlights how BGP confederations blend elements of both iBGP and eBGP to create a scalable yet logically consistent routing structure.

In operational practice, confederations are often deployed by large Internet service providers, content delivery networks, and multinational enterprises managing distributed backbones. The decision to implement a confederation is typically driven by network size, geographic distribution, administrative complexity, or a combination of these factors. By segmenting the network logically, organizations gain additional control over how internal routing is handled, leading to better scaling, clearer policy demarcation points, and improved troubleshooting capabilities.

Although confederations offer significant advantages, they also require careful design and planning. Engineers must consider the layout of sub-AS boundaries, the establishment of consistent policies between sub-ASes, and the potential interaction with external peers, route reflectors, and automation systems. Like any network design decision, confederations are most effective when implemented with a clear understanding of the organization's current and future scalability and policy requirements.

Ultimately, BGP confederations are a testament to the flexibility and extensibility of the Border Gateway Protocol. By enabling large autonomous systems to be logically segmented into smaller, independently managed units, confederations help overcome one of the fundamental scaling challenges of BGP, supporting the continued growth and evolution of global IP networks. They allow networks to maintain a unified external identity while benefiting internally from the operational simplicity of smaller routing domains, reinforcing BGP's role as the backbone protocol of the Internet.

Route Reflectors and iBGP Scaling

One of the most significant challenges faced by large-scale networks using the Border Gateway Protocol is the inherent scalability limitation imposed by the full mesh requirement of internal BGP. In a traditional iBGP environment, every router within an autonomous system running iBGP is expected to establish a direct peering session with every other iBGP-speaking router in the same AS. While this works effectively in small networks with a handful of routers, it quickly becomes unmanageable in larger networks. The number of required iBGP sessions grows exponentially as more routers are added, leading to increased memory usage, higher CPU loads, and operational complexity. To overcome this limitation, route reflectors were introduced as a mechanism to reduce the number of required iBGP sessions and make iBGP viable for networks of significant size.

Route reflectors fundamentally change the peering model of iBGP by allowing certain routers, designated as reflectors, to redistribute routes to other iBGP routers within the AS, known as clients. In a standard iBGP full-mesh configuration, when one iBGP router receives a route from an iBGP peer, it is not allowed to advertise that route to other iBGP peers due to the iBGP split-horizon rule. This rule was put in place to prevent routing loops within the autonomous system. However, when using route reflectors, this rule is relaxed. A route reflector is permitted to advertise iBGP-learned routes to its clients and to other route reflectors, significantly reducing the total number of iBGP sessions required.

The basic operation of a route reflector involves establishing iBGP sessions with multiple client routers and with other route reflectors in the network. The route reflector takes on the responsibility of redistributing routes learned from one client to other clients and peers. This reduces the number of peering sessions each client must maintain because clients only need to peer with their designated reflector or reflectors rather than maintaining a full mesh with every other iBGP-speaking router in the AS. For example, instead of requiring ten routers to establish forty-five individual iBGP sessions in a full mesh, a route reflector topology might reduce this number significantly by centralizing route distribution through one or two reflectors.

Route reflectors provide substantial operational and performance benefits. By reducing the number of iBGP sessions, they decrease router CPU utilization, lower memory consumption, and simplify configuration and maintenance. This scalability solution is particularly important for large service providers and enterprises with hundreds of routers distributed across multiple regions. Without route reflectors, such networks would face prohibitive complexity and resource consumption due to the sheer volume of iBGP sessions required under the full-mesh model.

Route reflector clusters are a common deployment pattern where a group of routers shares a route reflector. In this model, one or more routers act as route reflectors for a set of client routers, forming a logical grouping known as a cluster. Each cluster is identified by a unique cluster ID to prevent routing loops. When a route reflector advertises a route to another reflector, it appends its cluster ID to the BGP update. If a route reflector receives a route that already contains its own cluster ID, it will reject the update, preventing the route from being re-advertised to the same cluster and avoiding potential loops.

While route reflectors solve many scaling issues, they also introduce new design considerations and trade-offs. One of the primary concerns is the potential for suboptimal routing paths. In a full-mesh iBGP topology, all routers have a direct view of all other routers' routes, allowing for more informed routing decisions. However, in a route reflector environment, client routers depend on reflectors to receive route information, which may result in less visibility into alternative paths. This phenomenon, sometimes referred to as the hot-potato effect, occurs when routers forward traffic to the nearest egress point without considering the globally optimal path, potentially leading to inefficient use of network resources or higher latency paths.

To mitigate these issues, many networks deploy redundant or hierarchical route reflector designs. Redundancy is introduced by assigning multiple route reflectors to the same cluster, ensuring that if one reflector fails, clients can still receive routing updates from another reflector. Hierarchical designs may involve multiple tiers of route reflectors, with reflectors peering with higher-tier reflectors to ensure that route information is fully distributed throughout the network. This approach enhances both resilience and route visibility while maintaining the scalability benefits of the route reflector model.

Route reflectors also facilitate network segmentation by supporting separate clusters for different regions or business units within a single autonomous system. For instance, a multinational service provider might deploy distinct route reflector clusters for North America, Europe, and Asia, each optimized for regional traffic engineering and policy enforcement. This enables localized routing optimizations while still allowing global route propagation across cluster boundaries.

In modern networks, route reflectors play a critical role not only in traditional IP routing but also in the context of Multi-Protocol BGP (MP-BGP) environments. They are commonly used in MPLS Layer 3 VPN architectures, where route reflectors distribute VPNv4 and VPNv6 prefixes across provider edge routers (PEs). In this context, route reflectors help maintain the scalability of VPN services by efficiently propagating customer-specific routes within the service provider's backbone without overwhelming PEs with unnecessary session counts.

Despite their advantages, route reflectors require careful planning around convergence times and policy consistency. Improper placement or insufficient redundancy can introduce single points of failure, while inconsistent policies between route reflectors and clients can result in asymmetric routing or unintended traffic engineering outcomes. Operators must also ensure that route reflectors are properly integrated with the IGP to guarantee next-hop reachability for all distributed routes, as BGP relies on the IGP to resolve NEXT_HOP addresses.

As networks continue to scale and evolve, route reflectors remain a foundational technology that enables service providers, cloud operators, and enterprises to manage large and complex iBGP environments efficiently. Their role in reducing session count, facilitating hierarchical designs, and supporting modern services like MPLS VPNs underscores their importance in modern IP networks. Route reflectors embody the balance between scalability and operational simplicity, ensuring that even as networks grow in size and complexity, BGP remains a practical and reliable protocol for inter-domain routing.

BGP and Policy Control

The Border Gateway Protocol is not merely a mechanism for distributing routing information across autonomous systems; it is also a robust framework for implementing policy control within and between networks. One of the key features that sets BGP apart from interior routing protocols is its policy-driven nature, enabling network operators to enforce business rules, optimize traffic flows, and maintain security boundaries through routing decisions. The flexibility provided by BGP's policy mechanisms allows operators to go beyond purely technical considerations, integrating business logic into how routes are accepted, preferred, and propagated across the global Internet.

At its most fundamental level, policy control in BGP is about deciding which routes should be accepted from peers, which routes should be advertised to them, and which routes should be preferred when multiple paths exist to the same destination. BGP policies shape how an autonomous system interacts with its peers, upstream providers, customers, and the broader Internet. These policies are typically enforced using a combination of prefix filters, route maps, policy statements, and manipulation of BGP attributes such as LOCAL_PREF, MED, AS_PATH, and BGP communities.

One of the most common applications of BGP policy control is route filtering. Networks often apply inbound filters to routes received from external peers to limit the prefixes accepted into their routing tables. This serves multiple purposes: reducing unnecessary or undesirable routes, protecting against misconfigurations or malicious announcements, and ensuring routing tables remain efficient and manageable. For example, an ISP may only accept customer route advertisements for prefixes that the customer is authorized to announce, rejecting any unexpected or improperly scoped prefixes. Similarly, outbound filtering allows a network to control which prefixes it advertises to peers, preventing route leaks and reducing the risk of blackholing or routing instability on the Internet.

Beyond simple acceptance or rejection of routes, BGP policies are essential for influencing routing decisions through attribute manipulation. LOCAL_PREF, for instance, is widely used to control outbound traffic flows within an autonomous system. By assigning higher LOCAL_PREF values to preferred routes, network operators can ensure that traffic destined for external networks exits the AS through specific upstream providers or egress points. This capability is vital for multi-homed networks where optimizing cost, performance, or redundancy often requires directing traffic through selected links.

Manipulating the AS_PATH attribute is another common policy strategy, particularly for inbound traffic engineering. By prepending additional instances of their AS number to the AS_PATH of certain routes, networks can make these routes appear less attractive to remote peers. This technique encourages external networks to select alternative paths when routing traffic toward the AS, giving operators a way to balance inbound traffic loads or influence how traffic enters their network. AS_PATH prepending is often applied selectively, depending on the destination prefix or the specific peer receiving the advertisement.

MED, or MULTI_EXIT_DISC, is another attribute frequently used in BGP policy control. Although MED is primarily a hint for neighboring autonomous systems to prefer one ingress point over another, it enables more granular control in networks that maintain multiple connections with the same peer. By setting different MED values on route advertisements across multiple links, an AS can suggest preferred entry points for inbound traffic. While MED is considered after other attributes such as LOCAL_PREF and AS_PATH length during the BGP decision process, it still plays a crucial role in multi-exit environments, particularly when policies are agreed upon between cooperative peers.

BGP communities expand policy control by providing a flexible and scalable tagging mechanism for routes. Communities allow operators to encode additional routing instructions into BGP advertisements, which can then be interpreted by other routers to apply specific policies. For instance, a service provider might allow customers to tag routes with communities that influence how the provider advertises those routes to upstream providers or peers. A customer might request via community tags that certain routes only be advertised to specific regional peers or that LOCAL_PREF be adjusted within the provider's network. Communities thus enable customer-driven policy enforcement without requiring manual intervention from the provider's engineers on a per-prefix basis.

The combination of prefix filtering, attribute manipulation, and community-based policies allows network operators to build highly sophisticated routing strategies that align with business objectives. Policies can be designed to optimize costs by directing traffic through preferred providers, to enhance performance by prioritizing low-latency paths, or to improve resilience by ensuring traffic takes the most reliable routes during network failures. Moreover, BGP's policy mechanisms are critical for maintaining security on the Internet, allowing networks to enforce boundaries that prevent the propagation of unwanted or malicious routes.

In addition to traditional policy tools, modern networks are increasingly incorporating automation into BGP policy control. Configuration management systems, policy engines, and network orchestration platforms enable operators to dynamically adjust BGP policies in response to real-time network telemetry, traffic patterns, or external business factors. For example, a network might automatically reduce the LOCAL_PREF on routes learned from a provider experiencing performance degradation, rerouting outbound traffic through an alternative path with better metrics. Similarly, policies can be integrated into security response systems, allowing networks to dynamically blackhole routes under attack using BGP blackholing techniques combined with community tagging.

The enforcement of BGP policies is especially critical in environments where multiple administrative domains interact, such as Internet Exchange Points, multi-provider environments, and transit networks. Each AS involved in interconnection has its own interests and business priorities, and BGP policy control is the means by which these interests are protected and negotiated. Peering agreements often stipulate specific routing policies, such as restrictions on transiting traffic between third parties or requirements to honor MED values. The ability to implement these agreements effectively at the routing level ensures that business relationships are reflected in actual routing behavior.

Policy control within BGP also serves as a defense mechanism against common routing incidents, including route leaks and hijacks. By implementing strict inbound prefix filtering and validating routes based on Internet Routing Registries (IRRs) or Resource Public Key Infrastructure (RPKI) data, network operators can mitigate the risk of accepting unauthorized or misrouted prefixes. Additionally, outbound filtering helps prevent the accidental advertisement of internal or customer routes to external peers, preserving network security and global routing stability.

Ultimately, BGP's policy control capabilities are what allow it to serve as the Internet's de facto inter-domain routing protocol. Its flexibility enables networks to tailor routing behaviors to meet both technical requirements and business goals, providing a level of control that is unmatched by other routing protocols. The ability to influence how traffic flows across a complex and decentralized global network is a fundamental aspect of how the Internet operates today. Every route decision, every preference, and every filtering rule enforced by BGP is shaped by policy, reflecting the unique needs and priorities of the networks that comprise the Internet. The depth and breadth of BGP policy control are what empower network engineers to design, optimize, and secure the global routing system.

BGP Filtering Techniques

Border Gateway Protocol filtering is one of the most critical operational practices for maintaining routing stability, security, and efficiency on the Internet. As a policy-based protocol, BGP provides network operators with powerful tools to control which prefixes are accepted from and advertised to neighboring autonomous systems. Filtering techniques help prevent route leaks, mitigate the risk of route hijacks, reduce unnecessary routing information, and ensure compliance with both technical and business policies. Without the careful implementation of BGP filtering, networks risk propagating invalid or unauthorized routes that can lead to outages, blackholing, or routing inefficiencies on a local or global scale.

At its most basic level, BGP filtering involves controlling the flow of route advertisements between BGP peers. This control is applied both inbound, to restrict the routes a network accepts from its neighbors, and outbound, to limit which prefixes a network advertises to external peers or customers. Inbound filtering is essential for protecting the routing integrity of a network by validating external route advertisements, while outbound filtering ensures that sensitive or undesired internal routes do not leave the autonomous system.

One of the primary tools used in BGP filtering is the prefix list. Prefix lists allow network operators to define sets of IP prefixes that are either permitted or denied when matched against incoming or outgoing BGP updates. For example, an ISP may configure an inbound prefix list to accept only the IP prefixes that a customer has been authorized to announce, based on pre-negotiated agreements. Any unauthorized prefixes, or those outside the agreed-upon IP space, are denied by the prefix list and are not installed in the routing table. This prevents accidental or malicious announcements of incorrect or overly broad prefixes, such as the infamous incidents where an ISP accidentally advertised all of the Internet's IP space to its upstream providers.

Outbound prefix filtering serves a similarly important role by preventing a network from unintentionally advertising private IP address space, internal-only routes, or customer-specific prefixes to external peers. For instance, an ISP must ensure that RFC 1918 private address space, which is used internally and not routable on the global

Internet, is never advertised outside of its autonomous system. Outbound prefix filtering guarantees that only globally routable prefixes with proper authorization are shared with peers, maintaining the security and hygiene of the Internet's global routing system.

Route maps are another essential component of BGP filtering techniques. Unlike prefix lists, which match purely on IP addresses and prefix lengths, route maps provide greater flexibility by allowing operators to match and manipulate routes based on a combination of attributes, such as AS_PATH, BGP communities, LOCAL_PREF, and MED. A route map consists of a series of match and set statements, where match statements define the conditions under which a route is filtered or modified, and set statements specify the actions to take when a match occurs. For example, an inbound route map could match on a specific BGP community and reject the route if the community indicates that the route should not be accepted by the receiving network.

Route maps are often used in conjunction with prefix lists to apply more complex and nuanced filtering policies. For example, an inbound route map might accept only those prefixes that are part of a customer's allocated IP space and that also contain a specific community tag indicating they are production routes, while denying routes tagged for testing or backup purposes. This layered approach to filtering provides operators with fine-grained control over which routes are accepted and how they are treated upon receipt.

Another key filtering technique is AS_PATH filtering. The AS_PATH attribute records the autonomous systems that a route advertisement has traversed. By applying filters based on the contents of the AS_PATH, operators can enforce policies regarding which autonomous systems they are willing to accept routes from. For instance, a network might block routes that have transited through known hijacker ASes or reject routes with excessively long AS_PATHs to prevent route leaks and protect against instability. AS_PATH filters are also commonly used to enforce transit policies, such as preventing customer routes from being advertised to other customers in violation of peering agreements.

BGP community filtering is also widely used to implement more dynamic and scalable routing policies. Communities are tags that can be attached to BGP routes to indicate specific instructions or categorizations. Operators can filter routes based on these community values, accepting or denying routes according to the routing policies associated with those tags. For example, a network may use community filtering to honor blackhole requests from customers by only accepting and discarding routes tagged with a predefined blackhole community.

Filtering techniques extend beyond basic security and hygiene; they are also crucial for optimizing routing decisions. For example, networks may filter more-specific prefixes (also known as de-aggregation filtering) to reduce the number of routes in their routing tables and prevent routing churn. This is particularly relevant in large networks where excessive de-aggregation can overwhelm routers and degrade performance. By filtering prefixes with subnet masks that are too long, such as /24 or longer in IPv4, operators can enforce aggregation policies that promote more efficient use of routing resources.

While filtering is primarily used to control the flow of route advertisements, it is equally important in preventing the propagation of routing errors. Route leaks, in which an AS improperly advertises routes from one peer to another, often occur due to missing or misconfigured outbound filters. Strict filtering practices at the AS edge prevent such incidents by ensuring that customer or peer routes are only advertised according to defined business relationships and routing policies. For instance, a transit provider may configure outbound filters to ensure that customer prefixes are never advertised to other customers or peers unless explicitly allowed by policy.

Additionally, modern filtering techniques are increasingly being augmented by validation frameworks such as Resource Public Key Infrastructure (RPKI). By validating the origin AS of a prefix against cryptographically signed Route Origin Authorizations (ROAs), operators can automate parts of the filtering process and reduce the risk of accepting hijacked or misrouted prefixes. Networks that implement RPKI-based filtering can reject invalid routes before they enter the global routing system, improving security and routing reliability across the Internet.

Filtering in BGP is not a one-time activity but an ongoing operational responsibility. As networks grow, peering relationships evolve, and traffic patterns shift, operators must regularly review and update filtering policies to reflect current requirements. Misconfigured or outdated filters can have significant consequences, leading to route leaks, service outages, or reputational damage. Proper documentation, regular audits, and automated validation tools are essential for maintaining robust and effective filtering practices.

Ultimately, BGP filtering techniques form the foundation of safe and reliable routing operations. By leveraging tools such as prefix lists, route maps, AS_PATH filters, community filtering, and origin validation frameworks, network operators gain precise control over the flow of routing information in and out of their autonomous systems. These filtering techniques not only safeguard the stability of individual networks but also contribute to the security and resilience of the broader Internet, making them indispensable in modern network engineering.

Prefix Lists and Route Maps

In the world of BGP, where routing policies shape how networks communicate globally, two of the most essential tools for enforcing these policies are prefix lists and route maps. These mechanisms form the foundation for how network operators filter and manipulate routing information exchanged between autonomous systems. While BGP provides the protocol framework for sharing routing data, prefix lists and route maps give operators the power to enforce rules, manage security, optimize routing paths, and maintain the operational integrity of their networks. Understanding the role and application of both tools is crucial for engineers tasked with managing and securing complex BGP environments.

Prefix lists are primarily used for filtering BGP route advertisements based on IP prefixes. They allow administrators to define specific sets of IP address ranges, along with subnet mask conditions, to either permit or deny routes during the BGP update process. Unlike standard access control lists (ACLs), which were traditionally used for packet filtering, prefix lists are optimized for routing decisions and are capable of handling a wider range of IP matching conditions more efficiently. A prefix list entry typically specifies an IP prefix and a range of acceptable subnet mask lengths. For example, a prefix list might permit all subnets within 192.0.2.0/24 that have a mask length between /24 and /30 while denying all other prefixes.

The importance of prefix lists in routing control cannot be overstated. In inbound filtering, prefix lists help ensure that only authorized and expected routes are accepted from a peer or customer. This prevents incidents such as accidental advertisements of private address space or route leaks, which can lead to major Internet disruptions. On the outbound side, prefix lists ensure that a network only advertises specific prefixes to its peers, safeguarding internal or non-routable address space from leaking into the global routing system. In both cases, prefix lists act as a first line of defense, enforcing basic route filtering to comply with security and operational best practices.

While prefix lists focus on matching routes based on IP and subnet masks, route maps are far more flexible and provide a comprehensive framework for both filtering and policy enforcement. A route map consists of a series of statements, known as clauses, that define conditions (match statements) and actions (set statements). Match statements in a route map allow for filtering based on attributes beyond just prefixes. For example, routes can be matched based on AS_PATH length, BGP community tags, route origin, or specific MED values. Once a match is found, the set statements allow operators to modify routing attributes, such as changing the LOCAL_PREF, prepending the AS_PATH, or adjusting the MED before propagating the route.

The power of route maps lies in their ability to integrate multiple match conditions and policy actions into a single configuration block. This modular design enables network operators to build highly granular routing policies that align with complex technical and business requirements. For example, a route map could be designed to match on a specific IP prefix and a particular community tag and then apply AS_PATH prepending to de-preference the route before advertising it to a specific peer. Another use case could involve increasing LOCAL_PREF on certain customer routes within the AS to ensure that traffic exits the network through preferred upstream providers.

Route maps are not only used for filtering but also for route redistribution between routing protocols. In many networks, BGP is used alongside interior gateway protocols like OSPF or IS-IS. When redistributing routes from one protocol into another, route maps are used to filter and modify routes, controlling which prefixes are redistributed and how attributes such as metrics or tags are set during redistribution. This is particularly important in maintaining route summarization, preventing routing loops, and ensuring consistency between the internal and external routing domains.

When used together, prefix lists and route maps create a powerful combination for controlling routing behavior. Prefix lists often serve as components within route maps, forming part of the match criteria. For example, a route map might use a prefix list to match on specific IP blocks, followed by match conditions for communities or AS_PATH filters, and finally execute set statements to adjust attributes. This layered approach ensures that only carefully selected routes are accepted or advertised, and that those routes are properly manipulated according to the network's routing policies.

Another common practice is to apply prefix lists directly to BGP neighbor relationships, filtering routes during the BGP update process at the source. However, route maps provide more advanced filtering capabilities when networks require conditional logic or need to take actions beyond simply permitting or denying prefixes. For instance, route maps allow networks to implement policies such as limiting routes to specific peers, applying routing preferences for multi-homed customers, or managing blackhole routing policies by matching on community tags.

In larger networks, especially within Internet service providers and multinational enterprises, prefix lists and route maps are used to enforce routing policies on thousands of prefixes across dozens or hundreds of BGP sessions. In such environments, the scalability and maintainability of these tools become critical. Operators typically adopt structured naming conventions and modular designs for prefix lists and route maps to ensure clarity and simplify future modifications.

Automation frameworks and configuration management tools are often integrated to manage and deploy these policies consistently across large network footprints.

Additionally, the careful use of prefix lists and route maps plays a key role in network security. They prevent unauthorized route advertisements, help mitigate the risk of BGP hijacking, and protect the global routing system from instability. Networks that fail to implement proper filtering mechanisms are at a higher risk of causing or being impacted by routing anomalies, such as route leaks that can disrupt Internet traffic globally.

Modern best practices also recommend combining prefix lists and route maps with other validation systems, such as RPKI and BGP Maximum Prefix Limits, to create a defense-in-depth strategy. While prefix lists and route maps control the acceptance and modification of routing information, RPKI ensures that prefixes have valid origin authorizations, and maximum prefix limits prevent routers from accepting an excessive number of prefixes from a peer, which could otherwise exhaust router resources.

Ultimately, prefix lists and route maps form the operational foundation for controlling BGP behavior and enforcing routing policies. They empower network operators to filter unwanted routes, enforce business and technical agreements, and fine-tune routing attributes to optimize traffic flows. Whether used to manage simple peer-to-peer exchanges or to implement complex multi-domain routing architectures, these tools are indispensable in the daily management of BGP networks. Their proper implementation not only enhances the security and stability of individual networks but also contributes to the health and reliability of the broader Internet ecosystem.

The BGP Decision Process in Depth

The BGP decision process is at the heart of how the Internet routes traffic globally. While BGP is responsible for exchanging routing information between autonomous systems, it is the decision process that determines which route will be selected when multiple paths to the same destination are available. This selection is crucial because each route may represent a different commercial agreement, network performance, security posture, or physical topology. The BGP decision process is not a simple metric-based evaluation like other routing protocols; instead, it follows a series of clearly defined steps to ensure that the best route is chosen according to both technical and policy-driven criteria.

The process begins when a BGP router receives multiple route advertisements for the same destination prefix. The router must then compare these routes against one another, applying the decision-making rules in a strict sequence. The first step in the BGP decision process is to select the route with the highest weight. Weight is a Cisco-proprietary attribute, locally significant to the router, and is not advertised to other routers. A higher weight value will always take precedence, making it a powerful tool for influencing route selection on a single device. Network operators often use weight to enforce local policies or to ensure that certain routers favor specific paths.

If the weight is the same across all candidate routes, the next attribute BGP considers is the LOCAL_PREF. LOCAL_PREF is a well-known discretionary attribute that is shared among all routers within the same autonomous system. A route with a higher LOCAL_PREF value is preferred over those with lower values. This attribute is commonly used for outbound traffic engineering, allowing an autonomous system to choose preferred egress points to external networks. In multi-homed environments, administrators frequently manipulate LOCAL_PREF to direct traffic through lower-cost or higher-performance upstream providers.

Once LOCAL_PREF has been evaluated and if routes are still tied, BGP looks at the locally originated status of the routes. Routes that are originated by the local router, either via network statements, redistribution, or aggregate-address commands, are preferred over routes learned from peers. This rule favors locally sourced routes, reinforcing the operator's intention that locally originated prefixes should take precedence.

The next step in the process is to evaluate the AS_PATH length. The route with the shortest AS_PATH is selected, reflecting the traditional view that fewer autonomous system hops generally result in a more direct or efficient route. However, this is not always an indicator of the best performance path, which is why operators often manipulate AS_PATHs through prepending to influence upstream decisions. Despite this, AS_PATH length remains one of the most recognizable elements of BGP's decision logic and is critical in preventing routing loops.

After AS_PATH length, BGP evaluates the ORIGIN attribute. The ORIGIN indicates how the prefix was introduced into BGP, with three possible values: IGP, EGP, or INCOMPLETE. The protocol prefers routes with an IGP origin over EGP and INCOMPLETE origins, although in many modern networks, this attribute plays a minor role due to the dominance of BGP as the primary inter-domain routing protocol and the phasing out of the older EGP.

Following the origin check, BGP inspects the MED value. The MULTI_EXIT_DISC attribute serves as a suggestion to external neighbors regarding which link should be preferred when multiple entry points into the same AS exist. A lower MED value is preferred. Importantly, BGP only compares MED values between routes received from the same autonomous system by default. However, some networks choose to override this behavior by enabling MED comparison across all peers. MED is widely used in environments where two autonomous systems peer at multiple physical locations, allowing one AS to indicate which ingress points it prefers for specific prefixes.

In the event of a continued tie, BGP will then favor routes learned via eBGP over those learned via iBGP. This rule prioritizes external routes over internal advertisements, reflecting the typical design where eBGP-learned routes represent real external paths, whereas iBGP routes are usually internal redistributions of those external paths. This step helps maintain routing efficiency and ensures that traffic is not unnecessarily redirected within the local AS.

If the tie persists, BGP checks the lowest IGP metric to the BGP NEXT_HOP. This means that the router evaluates how close it is, in terms of internal IGP cost, to the next-hop IP address of the BGP route. The router will prefer the path with the lowest internal cost to reach the next-hop router, reinforcing the importance of good IGP design alongside BGP policies. This step is where the integration of BGP and the internal routing protocol becomes most evident, as internal metrics can influence the selection of external paths.

If multiple routes still remain equal, the router looks at the BGP router ID, selecting the path learned from the router with the lowest router ID. The router ID is a unique identifier assigned to each BGP-speaking router, often the highest IP address of a loopback interface or another configured address. In the highly unlikely case that the router IDs are also identical, BGP will break the tie by choosing the peer with the lowest IP address.

While this sequence may appear purely hierarchical and rigid, the flexibility of BGP comes from the ability of operators to influence multiple attributes simultaneously. For example, by setting both LOCAL_PREF and manipulating AS_PATH prepending, operators can fine-tune how their networks select outbound and inbound routes, aligning technical routing decisions with commercial and operational strategies. This capability makes BGP the most powerful inter-domain routing protocol, as it provides complete control over path selection.

Another important aspect to consider is that this decision process occurs independently on each router. This means that two routers in the same autonomous system might select different best paths for the same prefix, depending on their policies and network topology. This decentralized decision-making is one of the defining characteristics of BGP and contributes to its resilience and flexibility.

In practice, network operators also introduce route maps, prefix lists, and policy statements to further refine route choices before routes even reach the decision process. By filtering or modifying routes as they are received or sent, operators can influence which paths are even eligible to enter the decision process. Additionally, attributes like BGP communities can automate policy control, allowing routers to apply predefined actions to route advertisements based on community tags.

The BGP decision process, while procedural, is ultimately about striking a balance between technical metrics and administrative control. Each step reflects decades of operational experience and the evolving needs of the Internet, ensuring that autonomous systems can make informed decisions that align with their unique policies. The depth of the BGP decision process illustrates why BGP is not just a routing protocol but a comprehensive system for managing complex inter-network relationships across the globe.

BGP and Multi-Homing

Multi-homing is a critical strategy employed by organizations and service providers to improve network resilience, enhance performance, and increase control over traffic flows. At the core of multi-homing is the practice of connecting a single autonomous system to two or more upstream providers or peer networks. The Border Gateway Protocol is the essential enabler of multi-homing, providing the mechanisms needed to manage multiple external connections and make intelligent routing decisions across them. BGP gives networks the ability to select optimal paths, influence inbound and outbound traffic patterns, and ensure service continuity even in the event of link or provider failures.

A multi-homed network can range from a small enterprise that connects to two Internet service providers to a large content delivery network with dozens of global peers and transit providers. The common factor is the presence of multiple external BGP sessions, each representing a path into or out of the autonomous system. These multiple connections allow the network to achieve redundancy by maintaining alternative paths in case one provider or connection becomes unavailable. When configured properly, BGP automatically adapts to such failures by withdrawing affected routes and promoting alternative paths, ensuring that network services remain accessible to users and partners.

One of the key benefits of multi-homing is traffic engineering, the ability to influence how traffic enters and exits the network. On the outbound side, networks use BGP attributes such as LOCAL_PREF to control which upstream provider is preferred for specific traffic. For example, if an organization wants to prioritize sending traffic through Provider A due to lower costs or better performance, administrators can set a higher LOCAL_PREF value for routes learned from that provider. Conversely, Provider B might be used as a backup or for overflow traffic by assigning it a lower LOCAL_PREF. This approach allows the network to balance cost efficiency with performance needs, making real-time adjustments when conditions change.

On the inbound side, traffic engineering becomes more complex since it depends on influencing how external autonomous systems choose paths to reach the multi-homed network's prefixes. A common technique used to influence inbound traffic is AS_PATH prepending. By artificially lengthening the AS_PATH in route advertisements sent to a less preferred provider, the network can make that route less attractive to external peers, who typically prefer shorter AS_PATHs. For instance, a network might prepend its AS number three times when advertising to Provider B, signaling to other autonomous systems to prefer the shorter path through Provider A when sending traffic.

Another important tool in the multi-homing toolkit is the use of BGP communities. Many transit providers offer community-based policies that customers can use to tag route advertisements with instructions. A customer might use a provider's predefined community value to influence LOCAL_PREF inside the provider's network, or to control which peers or regions receive advertisements for specific prefixes. By using communities strategically, multi-homed networks can implement granular control over inbound traffic flows without relying solely on AS_PATH manipulation.

In multi-homed environments, ensuring consistent reachability and performance requires careful attention to route filtering and prefix advertisement. Networks must decide which prefixes to advertise to each provider and under what conditions. Some organizations choose to advertise their full set of prefixes to all upstream providers, ensuring full redundancy. Others might employ selective advertisement strategies, offering subsets of prefixes to specific providers based on geographical or business considerations. For example, a network might advertise its regional prefixes to a local provider and its global prefixes to a Tier 1 provider, optimizing for performance and cost within specific regions.

Multi-homing also has security implications. With multiple BGP sessions in place, the risk of route leaks or misconfigurations increases.

It is essential for networks to implement strict inbound and outbound filters on all BGP sessions. Inbound filtering ensures that only authorized and expected routes are accepted from upstream providers, while outbound filtering prevents private IP space or internal-only prefixes from being advertised to the global Internet. Employing prefix lists, route maps, and RPKI validation as part of the filtering strategy strengthens the integrity and security of the multi-homed environment.

Failover and redundancy are at the core of multi-homing's value proposition. In the event that one upstream provider experiences an outage or de-peering event, the multi-homed network can rely on its alternative provider(s) to maintain external connectivity. BGP's dynamic nature ensures that once a failure is detected—whether through BGP session loss, route withdrawals, or next-hop reachability issues—traffic is rerouted along the remaining available paths. This capability is critical for organizations where service continuity directly impacts customer satisfaction, revenue, and operational reliability.

In highly advanced multi-homed networks, route optimization platforms and BGP optimization appliances are sometimes deployed to automate traffic engineering decisions. These systems monitor network telemetry, performance metrics, and external routing changes, making dynamic adjustments to BGP policies to optimize cost and performance automatically. For example, a route optimization platform might shift traffic away from an upstream provider experiencing latency issues or congestion and redirect it through a better-performing alternative. This level of automation is particularly valuable in content delivery networks and large enterprises with global footprints where manual adjustments would be impractical.

The presence of multiple providers also introduces opportunities for commercial negotiation and cost control. By multi-homing, organizations gain leverage when negotiating service contracts, as they are no longer dependent on a single provider for all upstream connectivity. Providers may offer competitive pricing or additional service level guarantees to remain the preferred choice in the network's routing policies. This balance of technical flexibility and commercial advantage is one of the reasons multi-homing is a foundational design strategy for mission-critical networks.

Another dimension of multi-homing is its contribution to routing stability and global Internet resilience. Multi-homed networks often participate in the Internet ecosystem not only as consumers of transit services but also as contributors to routing redundancy and diversity. Their ability to select among multiple paths and adapt dynamically to external network conditions strengthens the Internet's decentralized nature. In times of large-scale disruptions—whether caused by natural disasters, geopolitical tensions, or infrastructure failures—multi-homed networks are often better positioned to maintain operational continuity and help route traffic through alternative paths, preserving global Internet functionality.

While multi-homing provides undeniable advantages, it also introduces operational complexities. Maintaining multiple BGP peerings, balancing traffic, preventing route leaks, and optimizing performance all require skilled engineering and ongoing monitoring. Documentation, automation, and consistent policy enforcement become vital to managing the increased complexity associated with multi-homing.

BGP, as the protocol enabling multi-homing, provides all the necessary tools to implement redundancy, optimize routing, and enforce sophisticated policies. Through careful manipulation of BGP attributes like LOCAL_PREF, AS_PATH, MED, and the use of communities, multi-homed networks can achieve their goals of resilience, flexibility, and performance optimization. Whether for an enterprise network with two upstream ISPs or a global content network connected to dozens of peers, BGP's capabilities make multi-homing one of the most strategic and effective designs in the modern Internet architecture.

BGP and Traffic Engineering

Traffic engineering is a core component of network operations that focuses on optimizing the performance, cost, and efficiency of traffic flows across complex networks. In the realm of inter-domain routing, the Border Gateway Protocol is the key tool for implementing traffic engineering strategies. While BGP was originally designed to provide reachability information between autonomous systems, it has evolved into a powerful mechanism that network operators use to shape both inbound and outbound traffic flows according to technical, business, and performance requirements. BGP's flexibility and policy-driven nature allow operators to influence how traffic enters and exits their networks, making it the cornerstone of traffic engineering on the Internet.

BGP-based traffic engineering typically addresses two distinct but related objectives: managing outbound traffic leaving a network and managing inbound traffic arriving from external sources. Outbound traffic engineering is generally easier to control because it is implemented entirely within an autonomous system. Network operators can directly influence which upstream provider or peer will be used to carry traffic toward a given destination by modifying attributes such as LOCAL_PREF, AS_PATH, and MED. For example, a multi-homed network connected to two transit providers can set a higher LOCAL_PREF on routes learned from Provider A, ensuring that internal routers prefer Provider A for outbound traffic. This allows the network to prioritize preferred providers based on cost agreements, performance metrics, or redundancy strategies.

Outbound traffic engineering can also leverage MED to influence routing decisions when dealing with peers or upstream providers that have multiple interconnection points. By advertising a lower MED value on specific links, an autonomous system can suggest preferred exit points for certain prefixes. Although MED is considered after LOCAL_PREF and AS_PATH length in the BGP decision process, it still plays an important role in fine-tuning traffic flows across multiple external interfaces, especially when both parties in the peering relationship agree to honor MED values.

The challenge of inbound traffic engineering, however, is more complex. Since inbound traffic decisions are made by external networks, the originating AS has limited direct control. Instead, network operators must influence how upstream providers and peers perceive available routes to reach their prefixes. One common technique for shaping inbound traffic is AS_PATH prepending. By artificially lengthening the AS_PATH in route advertisements sent to specific peers, the originating network can make that path less attractive to external networks that prefer shorter AS_PATHs. For instance, an autonomous system might prepend its AS number multiple times when advertising a prefix to a secondary provider, encouraging external networks to route traffic through the preferred, shorter path via a primary provider.

Another inbound traffic engineering technique involves prefix de-aggregation. By advertising more specific prefixes to certain providers or peers, a network can exert finer control over how traffic destined for its IP space enters the network. For example, a network might advertise a /16 prefix to all providers while selectively advertising more specific /24 prefixes to certain providers to steer traffic for those smaller subnets through desired ingress points. This tactic enables geographic or service-specific optimizations, such as directing traffic to a nearby data center or to a location with available capacity.

BGP communities further enhance traffic engineering capabilities by allowing networks to convey routing preferences to external peers in a scalable and automated way. Many transit providers and Internet exchanges support predefined community values that customers can use to request specific behaviors, such as adjusting LOCAL_PREF, limiting route propagation to certain regions, or applying AS_PATH prepending. For example, a customer might tag routes with a community that tells the upstream provider to advertise those routes only to North American peers, thereby reducing unwanted traffic from other regions and improving regional performance.

In addition to controlling how routes are advertised externally, BGP traffic engineering also plays a vital role internally within large autonomous systems. Enterprises and service providers often deploy iBGP policies to manage how traffic exits their networks toward external peers. Route reflectors, LOCAL_PREF adjustments, and IGP metric tuning toward next-hop addresses are common techniques used to optimize egress selection for outbound traffic. For example, adjusting the IGP cost to the next-hop IP address can influence BGP's route selection process when LOCAL_PREF and AS_PATH values are equal, ensuring that traffic exits via the nearest or most cost-effective border router.

BGP traffic engineering is not limited to performance optimization; it is also essential for balancing cost structures and meeting contractual obligations. Multi-homed organizations with diverse provider relationships often use BGP policies to ensure that traffic is balanced according to agreed-upon bandwidth commitments or pricing models. A network might send a greater share of its outbound traffic through a lower-cost provider while retaining higher-cost providers for redundancy and failover purposes. Similarly, traffic engineering can be applied to ensure that certain classes of traffic, such as critical application flows or customer-specific services, are routed through high-priority paths with better latency or reliability characteristics.

The dynamic nature of Internet traffic patterns also means that traffic engineering is not a one-time configuration task but an ongoing process. Network operators must continuously monitor network conditions, traffic volumes, and performance metrics to adjust BGP policies as necessary. Automation and network optimization platforms are increasingly used to aid in this process. These platforms can collect telemetry from network devices, analyze traffic flow data, and adjust BGP attributes programmatically to respond to real-time conditions. For example, if a particular upstream provider begins experiencing increased latency or packet loss, the automation platform can reduce the LOCAL_PREF associated with that provider's routes, shifting outbound traffic to an alternative path with better performance.

In MPLS and VPN environments, BGP traffic engineering plays an even broader role by interacting with additional technologies such as MPLS label switching and VRFs (Virtual Routing and Forwarding instances). In these environments, BGP distributes VPNv4 or VPNv6 routes between provider edge routers, and route distinguishers, route targets, and extended communities are used to define customer-specific traffic engineering policies. Service providers often apply different import and export policies to control how traffic is routed within and between VPNs, ensuring that service-level agreements and customer isolation requirements are met.

Security also intersects with BGP traffic engineering. By enforcing strict filtering policies alongside traffic engineering policies, network operators can protect their networks from routing anomalies, such as prefix hijacking or route leaks. Communities can be used to prevent certain routes from being advertised beyond specific regions or providers, while prefix filtering ensures that internal or private IP space is never accidentally advertised to the global Internet.

In large-scale networks, traffic engineering is not just a matter of routing efficiency; it also has direct financial and business implications. Efficient traffic engineering reduces operational costs, optimizes resource utilization, improves user experience through reduced latency and packet loss, and helps maintain contractual compliance with upstream providers and customers. Through BGP's flexible attribute system and rich policy enforcement capabilities, networks gain the tools needed to steer traffic intelligently across the constantly shifting topology of the Internet. From managing simple multi-homed edge connections to optimizing the traffic flows of a global backbone network, BGP remains the central component for traffic engineering strategies in today's interconnected world.

BGP Route Aggregation

BGP route aggregation is a fundamental technique used to reduce the size of routing tables and improve the efficiency and scalability of inter-domain routing. As the Internet has grown, so has the number of IP prefixes advertised by networks worldwide. Without effective aggregation, routers would be required to store and process millions of individual routes, placing unnecessary strain on hardware and making the global routing system less stable and more prone to inefficiencies. Route aggregation addresses this challenge by consolidating multiple, more specific IP prefixes into a single, broader summary route. This summarized route represents all the individual subnets it encompasses, allowing network operators to advertise fewer routes without sacrificing connectivity.

At its core, aggregation in BGP is about optimizing how routing information is shared between autonomous systems. For example, if an organization owns the address space 192.0.2.0/24 and internally subdivides it into multiple smaller subnets such as 192.0.2.0/26, 192.0.2.64/26, and 192.0.2.128/26, these subnets can be advertised as individual routes or as a single aggregated prefix, 192.0.2.0/24, to external peers. By advertising the summarized route instead of the more specific prefixes, the network reduces the number of entries in external routers' tables, streamlining the global routing system.

BGP supports aggregation through the aggregate-address command, which is configured on routers to generate summary routes based on the presence of specific, more detailed routes in the BGP table. The router creates an aggregate route and can optionally suppress the advertisement of the more specific component routes to external peers. This process helps ensure that external networks see only the summarized route, while the internal network maintains full visibility of the more granular subnets for detailed traffic engineering and routing purposes.

One key consideration in BGP route aggregation is the handling of attributes and policies. When multiple prefixes are aggregated into a single summarized route, attributes like AS_PATH, MED, and BGP communities may be lost or require modification. Because aggregated routes no longer directly reference the original advertisements, care must be taken to ensure that important routing policies are not unintentionally bypassed. For instance, if an organization aggregates multiple customer prefixes into a single route, it may need to apply common policies—such as AS_PATH prepending or setting specific BGP communities—at the aggregate level to preserve intended routing behavior.

The atomic aggregate attribute is an important part of the BGP aggregation process. When a router performs aggregation, it may include the atomic aggregate attribute in the BGP update to signal that the summarized route may no longer fully reflect the routing information contained within the more specific prefixes. This attribute informs receiving routers that the summarized route is a simplification and that some path information from the individual routes has been lost. Although modern networks sometimes disregard the atomic aggregate attribute, it still plays a role in helping downstream routers understand the context of the aggregate route.

The aggregator attribute is often used alongside atomic aggregate to provide additional transparency. The aggregator attribute specifies the AS number and router ID of the router that performed the aggregation. This information can assist in troubleshooting and network diagnostics by identifying where in the network the aggregation occurred and which autonomous system performed it.

Route aggregation also plays a vital role in preventing unnecessary global route propagation and reducing routing churn. Without aggregation, networks that de-aggregate their prefixes excessively could contribute to bloating the global BGP table, resulting in longer convergence times during network events, higher CPU usage, and memory strain on routers worldwide. By summarizing prefixes whenever possible, organizations contribute to the collective stability and efficiency of the Internet.

Another advantage of aggregation is its positive impact on traffic management and security. Aggregation can limit the exposure of internal network structures to external entities by masking the details of how IP address blocks are subdivided internally. This abstraction provides a layer of operational security and simplifies routing advertisements. Moreover, in failure scenarios, proper aggregation helps mitigate routing table instability. For instance, if a network loses one of several smaller prefixes due to a localized outage, the aggregated route may continue to advertise uninterrupted reachability for the larger summarized prefix, preserving external routing continuity.

However, aggregation must be implemented carefully to avoid unintended consequences. Improper or overly aggressive aggregation can create routing black holes if traffic is forwarded toward an aggregate route for which no specific internal route exists. To mitigate this risk, operators typically ensure that the summarized prefixes correspond to actual reachable subnets within their network. Null routes, or discard routes, are often configured for aggregate prefixes to ensure that traffic destined for unused portions of the summarized range is dropped rather than causing routing loops or instability.

In large-scale service provider environments, route aggregation is critical for managing backbone and customer-facing routers. Tier 1 ISPs and regional providers often aggregate customer prefixes before advertising them to upstream peers or other parts of their backbone, reducing the burden on core routers and improving route propagation efficiency. This practice also supports better traffic engineering and policy enforcement, as summarized routes can be combined with routing policies applied to specific regions, services, or customer classes.

Aggregation is also prevalent in MPLS Layer 3 VPN networks, where service providers may aggregate VPN prefixes before distributing them across their backbone using MP-BGP. This approach helps manage the scale of VPN route tables, particularly when supporting large numbers of customers with diverse prefix sets.

The decision to aggregate routes often balances operational efficiency with the need for precise routing control. In some cases, organizations may choose not to aggregate certain prefixes if doing so would limit their ability to engineer inbound traffic or influence routing decisions from external autonomous systems. For example, in situations where inbound traffic engineering relies on de-aggregated prefixes and selective advertisement to upstream providers, full aggregation may conflict with these traffic management goals.

Ultimately, BGP route aggregation is one of the most valuable techniques for maintaining the scalability and stability of the Internet. It reduces the size of global and local routing tables, enhances router performance, and supports the efficient distribution of routing information between autonomous systems. Properly implemented, aggregation helps networks achieve a balance between simplification and routing control, contributing to the operational health of both the local network and the broader Internet. Through aggregation, BGP demonstrates its power not only as a routing protocol but also as a tool for responsible network stewardship, ensuring that the Internet can continue to scale and operate efficiently as it grows.

BGP and MPLS VPNs

The combination of BGP and MPLS has revolutionized how service providers deliver secure, scalable, and highly customizable Virtual Private Network (VPN) services to customers. MPLS VPNs, particularly Layer 3 VPNs, use Multiprotocol BGP (MP-BGP) in conjunction with MPLS to enable the separation of customer traffic over a shared service provider backbone. This architecture allows multiple customer networks to coexist on the same physical infrastructure without interfering with one another, while still maintaining routing and security isolation between customers. MP-BGP provides the signaling mechanism that makes this possible, while MPLS is responsible for forwarding packets across the backbone with high performance and flexibility.

At the core of this design is the use of BGP to carry customer-specific routing information between Provider Edge (PE) routers. In a traditional IP routing model, customer routes would be advertised using an Interior Gateway Protocol (IGP) or simple eBGP between edge routers. However, MPLS VPNs require a more scalable and flexible solution. MP-BGP, as defined in RFC 4364, extends the traditional BGP protocol by supporting additional address families beyond IPv4, including VPNv4 and VPNv6. These address families allow PE routers to exchange customer routes that include additional identifiers, such as Route Distinguishers (RDs), which make each customer's prefixes globally unique within the provider's network.

When a customer route is learned by a PE router, it is imported into a Virtual Routing and Forwarding (VRF) instance, which serves as a dedicated routing table for that customer. The PE router then uses MP-BGP to advertise the route to other PE routers within the provider's backbone. The advertisement includes the customer's IP prefix, the RD, and a Route Target (RT), which is a BGP extended community used to control route import and export policies between VRFs. The Route Target mechanism allows operators to selectively import routes into specific VRFs, enabling granular control over which customer sites can communicate with each other.

MPLS provides the underlying transport layer for the VPN service. When a PE router advertises a VPN route via MP-BGP, it also associates the route with a label that will be used to forward traffic across the provider's MPLS core. When a packet destined for a customer's VPN arrives at a PE router, the router pushes one or more MPLS labels onto the packet. The outer label is used by the MPLS core to forward the packet across the backbone toward the destination PE router, while the inner label identifies the specific VPN on the destination PE. Upon reaching the destination PE router, the outer label is removed, and the inner label directs the router to forward the packet according to the correct VRF, ensuring that the traffic is kept isolated from other customers' data.

This architecture enables significant scalability benefits. Since PE routers use MP-BGP to share customer routes, the provider's core routers (P routers) do not need to maintain any customer-specific routing information. P routers simply perform MPLS label switching based on the outer MPLS label, allowing the core to remain simple and highly scalable. This separation between the control plane (BGP) and the data plane (MPLS) is one of the primary reasons MPLS VPNs have become the preferred solution for service providers offering enterprise-grade VPN services.

The integration of BGP into MPLS VPNs also provides powerful traffic engineering capabilities. By leveraging MPLS Traffic Engineering (MPLS-TE) and Constraint-Based Routing Label Distribution Protocol (CR-LDP) or RSVP-TE, service providers can influence how labeled packets traverse their network, optimizing resource utilization and meeting specific performance objectives such as latency or bandwidth guarantees. Additionally, by manipulating BGP attributes such as MED, LOCAL_PREF, and communities, providers can implement detailed policies that shape inter-site traffic flows across their backbone.

Security is another advantage of the BGP/MPLS VPN model. Each customer's traffic is logically isolated within its own VRF and is carried across the MPLS core using labels that prevent mixing with other customers' data. Unlike traditional IP-based VPNs that rely on IPsec tunnels between customer sites, MPLS VPNs offer a more integrated approach to traffic segregation and often result in lower latency and simplified management for service providers and customers alike. Furthermore, because MPLS VPNs operate at Layer 3, service providers can also offer value-added services such as network address translation (NAT), firewalling, and quality of service (QoS) policies directly within the VRF instances.

One of the key operational benefits of using MP-BGP in MPLS VPNs is the flexibility it provides in designing complex VPN topologies. For example, providers can create hub-and-spoke VPNs, where branch offices communicate only through a central headquarters site, or fully meshed VPNs, where all sites can communicate directly with one another. By carefully controlling which Route Targets are imported into each VRF, network engineers can tailor routing behaviors to meet customer requirements without modifying the underlying MPLS core.

Inter-provider VPN services are also enabled by the combination of BGP and MPLS. In scenarios where two service providers cooperate to extend VPN services across their respective networks, MP-BGP allows them to exchange VPN routing information securely and efficiently. This is accomplished using an Inter-AS model, where ASBRs (Autonomous System Border Routers) exchange VPNv4 or VPNv6 routes and labels across AS boundaries, enabling seamless VPN connectivity between customers with geographically dispersed sites across different service providers' networks.

The use of BGP and MPLS in VPNs has also paved the way for advanced services such as Layer 3 MPLS VPN Multicast. By integrating multicast routing protocols like PIM with MPLS and MP-BGP extensions, providers can offer multicast services within VPNs while maintaining traffic isolation and scalability. This is particularly valuable for industries such as financial services, where real-time data distribution to multiple branch offices is critical.

Additionally, the standardization of BGP/MPLS VPNs has allowed for broad interoperability between different vendors' equipment, promoting competition and innovation in the service provider market. As a result, enterprises benefit from a wide range of choices when selecting VPN providers, as well as from improved reliability and global reach.

From an operational standpoint, the deployment of BGP/MPLS VPNs requires a solid understanding of both BGP and MPLS principles. Network engineers must be adept at configuring VRFs, defining import and export Route Targets, implementing route maps for fine-grained policy control, and troubleshooting BGP sessions across PE routers. The combination of control plane policies and data plane label switching creates a powerful, but also complex, routing environment that demands careful planning and regular monitoring.

Ultimately, the integration of BGP with MPLS VPNs has provided service providers and large enterprises with a scalable, secure, and highly customizable solution for delivering private network services over a shared infrastructure. It demonstrates how BGP continues to evolve beyond its original role as the Internet's routing protocol, proving itself as a versatile and essential tool in the delivery of modern IP services. As networks continue to grow and customer demands for flexibility and security increase, the combination of BGP and MPLS remains a cornerstone technology for enabling robust and scalable VPN architectures worldwide.

The Role of BGP in Data Centers

In modern data centers, Border Gateway Protocol plays an increasingly critical role beyond its traditional use as the backbone routing protocol of the Internet. As data center architectures have evolved to meet the demands of cloud computing, massive scale, and highly available applications, BGP has emerged as a key protocol not only for external connectivity but also for managing routing within the data center fabric itself. While data centers have historically relied on Interior Gateway Protocols like OSPF and IS-IS for internal routing, the rise of large-scale, multi-tenant environments and software-defined networking has led to BGP becoming the preferred choice in many next-generation data center designs.

One of the reasons BGP is favored within data centers is its scalability. Data centers can host thousands of servers, virtual machines, and containers, all of which require efficient and scalable routing. BGP's ability to manage a vast number of routes without overwhelming the control plane or causing excessive CPU utilization on switches and routers makes it well-suited for large-scale environments. Unlike traditional IGPs, which rely on frequent link-state advertisements and can struggle under the weight of large topologies, BGP's path vector approach and policy-driven routing allow operators to scale networks horizontally while maintaining operational stability.

Another advantage of using BGP in data centers is its policy control. In large, multi-tenant environments where applications and services may require different routing preferences, BGP provides the flexibility to apply granular policies at the edge of the network and within the data center fabric. Operators can use attributes such as LOCAL_PREF, MED, AS_PATH prepending, and BGP communities to influence routing decisions based on business or performance objectives. For example, traffic from specific tenants may be routed through preferred network paths or given higher priority when exiting the data center to external destinations.

BGP's use in modern data centers is also closely tied to the adoption of spine-leaf architectures. In spine-leaf designs, leaf switches provide connectivity to servers and tenant devices, while spine switches act as the high-speed core, interconnecting all leaf switches. BGP is frequently used between leaf and spine switches to establish a simple yet highly scalable routing protocol. By running iBGP or eBGP sessions between these switches, operators eliminate the need for complex IGP configurations and simplify convergence across the fabric. Each leaf switch establishes BGP sessions with every spine switch, creating a resilient and load-balanced routing environment that can handle both east-west (intra-data center) and north-south (external) traffic efficiently.

Furthermore, many hyperscale cloud providers and large enterprises deploy BGP in an eBGP-only data center fabric, where each switch is treated as an autonomous system or sub-AS. This design enables the use of eBGP's simpler loop prevention mechanisms and allows for faster convergence compared to traditional iBGP with full-mesh or route reflector designs. The adoption of eBGP-only fabrics also aligns well with automation and zero-touch provisioning models, where configuration simplicity is paramount for deploying and scaling data center infrastructure rapidly.

BGP's extensibility has also made it a foundational component of emerging data center technologies such as EVPN (Ethernet VPN) and VXLAN. EVPN, when combined with VXLAN, provides a control plane for layer 2 and layer 3 services over an IP fabric. In this model, BGP carries MAC and IP address reachability information between VXLAN Tunnel Endpoints (VTEPs), enabling seamless layer 2 and layer 3 connectivity across the data center fabric. This approach solves many of the limitations of traditional layer 2 networking, such as broadcast domain scaling and spanning tree convergence issues, by replacing them with BGP-driven control and MPLS-like efficiency.

The role of BGP in facilitating data center interconnects (DCIs) has also expanded significantly. Organizations operating multiple geographically distributed data centers use BGP to exchange routing information between sites, enabling seamless traffic flow across regions. Whether implemented over MPLS, direct dark fiber, or through IPsec tunnels over the Internet, BGP provides the routing intelligence required to ensure application availability, disaster recovery, and business continuity. Furthermore, when combined with MPLS VPN or EVPN overlays, BGP enables multi-site tenants to operate as if their resources were in a single, contiguous data center, simplifying management and reducing complexity.

In hybrid cloud architectures, where enterprises extend their on-premises data centers to public cloud providers, BGP continues to serve as the protocol of choice for connecting with cloud service providers. Most public clouds support BGP peering for direct connections, such as AWS Direct Connect, Azure ExpressRoute, and Google Cloud Interconnect. These connections enable dynamic route exchange between the enterprise data center and the cloud provider, allowing seamless workload migration, failover, and hybrid application delivery. BGP's ability to carry policy attributes, automate failover, and manage routing preferences in these environments is vital to ensuring service reliability and performance.

Operationally, BGP's deterministic behavior and control plane stability provide additional benefits within data centers. The ability to control route advertisement and acceptance via prefix lists, route maps, and community-based policies gives operators confidence in maintaining routing consistency even as data center networks grow and change. BGP also supports graceful restart and fast reroute mechanisms that minimize downtime during maintenance or network failures, critical features for data centers hosting mission-critical applications and services.

Security is another area where BGP adds value to data center operations. BGP's policy control can be leveraged to enforce tenant isolation, restrict unauthorized route propagation, and prevent routing anomalies such as route leaks or hijacks. Furthermore, when combined with infrastructure security frameworks such as RPKI or maximum prefix limits, BGP deployments in data centers can be hardened against common routing threats.

BGP's ability to integrate with network automation tools further enhances its role in modern data centers. Configuration management systems and automation frameworks can dynamically update BGP policies and peerings, enabling rapid deployment of new services and seamless scaling of existing workloads. Network engineers can automate route redistribution, community tagging, and failover policies through API-driven controllers, reducing the potential for human error and accelerating the deployment cycle.

As data centers continue to evolve toward more cloud-native, microservices-based architectures, the importance of BGP is likely to grow. The protocol's ability to handle massive routing tables, support multi-tenant designs, and integrate with overlay technologies like VXLAN and EVPN makes it a cornerstone of modern data center networking. By enabling both flexibility and control, BGP allows network architects to build infrastructures that meet the demands of today's hyper-connected, high-availability environments. Whether used within a single data center fabric or across a global network of interconnected facilities, BGP has become essential for delivering scalable, resilient, and efficient routing solutions in the modern data center.

BGP and Cloud Networking

The rise of cloud computing has transformed how organizations design and operate their networks. At the center of this transformation is the Border Gateway Protocol, which plays a crucial role in connecting enterprise networks to cloud service providers and in enabling the highly dynamic, distributed nature of cloud architectures. While BGP was originally designed to route traffic between autonomous systems on the public Internet, it has become equally essential in modern cloud networking, supporting everything from hybrid cloud deployments to multi-cloud architectures and global content distribution networks. As workloads have shifted from centralized data centers to distributed cloud regions and edge locations, BGP's scalability and policy-driven control have made it the de facto protocol for managing routing across this expanded digital landscape.

One of the most significant applications of BGP in cloud networking is its role in hybrid cloud environments, where enterprises extend their private networks to connect with public cloud services such as Amazon Web Services, Microsoft Azure, Google Cloud Platform, and others. Cloud providers typically offer dedicated private connectivity services, such as AWS Direct Connect, Azure ExpressRoute, or Google Cloud Interconnect, which allow organizations to establish high-bandwidth, low-latency links between on-premises data centers and cloud provider infrastructure. These services rely on BGP to dynamically exchange routing information between the enterprise's autonomous system and the cloud provider's network. By automating route advertisement and withdrawal, BGP enables seamless failover between multiple cloud regions or direct connection endpoints, ensuring high availability for mission-critical applications.

BGP also facilitates the dynamic nature of cloud resources. In traditional data center environments, IP address assignments and routing paths are relatively static, but in the cloud, virtual machines, containers, and services are frequently created, moved, and terminated across multiple regions and availability zones. BGP allows cloud providers to advertise updated prefixes as services scale or migrate, enabling enterprise networks to adapt dynamically without manual reconfiguration. This dynamic routing model is particularly valuable for global organizations that require agile network infrastructures capable of responding to changing application demands and regional traffic shifts.

In multi-cloud architectures, where organizations leverage services from more than one public cloud provider, BGP provides a unified mechanism for interconnecting disparate environments. Enterprises may establish BGP peering sessions with multiple cloud providers through dedicated links or through carrier-neutral colocation facilities acting as cloud exchange points. By doing so, they can route traffic intelligently between cloud platforms, optimize latency-sensitive applications, and ensure redundancy. BGP's policy-driven routing model allows organizations to apply traffic engineering strategies across clouds, such as preferring one cloud provider over another for specific workloads based on cost, performance, or compliance requirements.

BGP communities are heavily used in cloud networking to implement granular routing policies. Cloud providers often define well-known communities that customers can use to control route propagation and path selection within the provider's network. For example, customers might apply community tags to indicate that certain prefixes should only be advertised to specific cloud regions or to influence LOCAL_PREF values within the provider's internal BGP infrastructure. This approach allows enterprises to optimize how their traffic is handled once inside the cloud, improving application performance and cost efficiency.

Another critical application of BGP in cloud networking is in supporting global content delivery networks (CDNs) and distributed edge computing infrastructures. CDNs rely on a network of geographically dispersed edge nodes to deliver content to end-users with minimal latency. These edge nodes often establish BGP sessions with multiple upstream providers, Internet exchanges, or regional ISPs to ensure optimal traffic paths for end-user requests. BGP allows CDNs to steer traffic based on real-time network conditions, advertise or withdraw prefixes dynamically based on server load or availability, and manage complex peering relationships with other networks globally.

Cloud-native services and technologies, such as Kubernetes, service meshes, and containerized microservices, have further highlighted BGP's relevance in cloud networking. Projects like MetalLB, a popular load-balancer solution for Kubernetes, use BGP to advertise service IPs from within a Kubernetes cluster to upstream routers or external networks. This allows workloads running inside the cluster to be accessible from outside the cloud infrastructure using standard routing protocols. BGP's ability to integrate seamlessly with these modern, distributed application frameworks underscores its importance in facilitating connectivity in cloud-native environments.

In addition to external connectivity, BGP is also leveraged inside cloud providers' own infrastructures. Hyperscale providers operate massive internal networks with thousands of routers and switches, spanning global regions and availability zones. Within these networks, BGP is often used as the control plane for large-scale IP fabrics, allowing providers to manage route propagation efficiently, apply routing policies for service isolation, and ensure rapid convergence in response to network changes or failures. The flexibility of BGP enables cloud providers to support multi-tenant environments while delivering highly available services to millions of customers worldwide.

The role of BGP in disaster recovery and high-availability cloud architectures is also significant. Enterprises often configure BGP-based routing policies to prioritize primary cloud regions while maintaining backup connections to secondary regions. In the event of a regional outage or service disruption, BGP automatically withdraws unavailable routes and shifts traffic to alternative paths. This failover capability is essential for businesses operating mission-critical workloads that require maximum uptime and minimal disruption.

Security is another key consideration where BGP's capabilities enhance cloud networking. Enterprises and cloud providers use BGP route filtering, prefix lists, and maximum prefix limits to ensure that only valid and authorized routes are exchanged between networks. In hybrid and multi-cloud environments, strict BGP policy enforcement helps prevent accidental route leaks, hijacks, or misconfigurations that could impact routing stability. The adoption of RPKI (Resource Public Key Infrastructure) by many cloud providers further strengthens the security posture of BGP sessions by enabling route origin validation.

Automation has also become a driving factor behind BGP's growing role in cloud networking. Modern infrastructure-as-code tools and orchestration platforms allow organizations to automate BGP session creation, route filtering, and traffic engineering policies. This capability is particularly important in DevOps and cloud-native workflows, where rapid deployment cycles and dynamic scaling require network configurations to adjust automatically without human intervention.

BGP's extensibility, flexibility, and interoperability with cloud platforms have made it a critical enabler of today's distributed, highly resilient cloud ecosystems. Whether used to manage connectivity between on-premises networks and public clouds, to integrate multiple cloud environments, or to build the global backbone of cloud providers themselves, BGP continues to provide the routing intelligence required to ensure performance, availability, and control. As organizations increasingly adopt hybrid and multi-cloud strategies, BGP's role as the backbone of cloud networking will only grow in significance, reinforcing its status as one of the most important protocols powering the modern Internet.

BGP Security: Threats and Risks

While the Border Gateway Protocol is the backbone of the global Internet, enabling autonomous systems to exchange routing information, its original design did not prioritize security. BGP was created in a more trusted environment, during a time when the Internet was relatively small and cooperative. As the Internet has expanded to include thousands of autonomous systems operated by commercial entities, governments, and organizations worldwide, the protocol has faced increasing security challenges. The absence of native authentication and route validation mechanisms has exposed BGP to a variety of threats, including route hijacking, route leaks, session hijacking, and denial-of-service (DoS) attacks. These vulnerabilities can have severe consequences, from traffic interception and blackholing to widespread Internet outages.

One of the most concerning BGP threats is route hijacking. In a route hijack scenario, a malicious or misconfigured autonomous system advertises IP prefixes that it does not legitimately own or control. When other networks receive these unauthorized advertisements, they may update their routing tables and send traffic to the hijacker's network instead of the intended destination. This can result in the diversion of traffic to an attacker, where it may be inspected, modified, or dropped entirely. Route hijacks can affect a single IP prefix or large portions of the Internet's address space, depending on the scope of the unauthorized advertisements. Several high-profile incidents have demonstrated the destructive impact of route hijacking, causing traffic destined for major online services to be redirected, sometimes for hours.

Closely related to hijacking is the issue of route leaks. A route leak occurs when an autonomous system incorrectly announces routes learned from one peer or provider to another peer or provider in violation of standard routing policies. For example, a customer network might improperly advertise Internet-wide routes learned from one upstream provider to another provider or peer. This creates unintended routing paths that can cause traffic to take suboptimal or insecure routes, leading to instability and degraded performance. In severe cases, route leaks can result in large segments of Internet traffic flowing through networks not intended to carry that traffic, exposing data to potential interception or surveillance.

BGP session hijacking represents another serious threat. In this type of attack, an adversary takes over an established BGP session between two legitimate routers by injecting malicious TCP packets with correct sequence numbers. Once the session is hijacked, the attacker can inject, modify, or withdraw BGP routes. This can lead to traffic redirection, blackholing, or manipulation of routing tables on a broader scale. Session hijacking is particularly dangerous because it allows attackers to assume the identity of a trusted BGP peer, making their injected routes appear legitimate to neighboring routers.

Denial-of-service attacks also target BGP infrastructure. BGP routers can be overwhelmed with illegitimate or malformed BGP updates, leading to excessive CPU utilization and memory exhaustion. Attackers may flood a router with bogus route advertisements, causing the device to crash or become unresponsive. Additionally, attackers can exploit the TCP-based nature of BGP sessions by launching SYN flood attacks against the TCP port used for BGP (port 179), preventing legitimate sessions from being established or maintained. A successful DoS attack on a key BGP router within a service provider's network can disrupt routing for large segments of the Internet.

BGP also faces threats related to configuration errors and human mistakes. Misconfigurations, such as accidentally advertising internal prefixes to external peers or failing to implement proper route filtering, are common and have led to significant outages. For example, if an ISP mistakenly advertises its full routing table to a customer, the customer could propagate those routes to the wider Internet, creating a route leak. Such events often occur due to a lack of rigorous filtering policies or incomplete automation and change control processes within networks.

The lack of native cryptographic protection within BGP exacerbates these risks. By default, BGP sessions rely on TCP for transport and do not include built-in encryption or authentication. While many networks implement TCP MD5 authentication to protect BGP sessions against spoofed TCP segments, this mechanism provides only basic protection and does not address other vulnerabilities, such as route hijacking or leaks. Additionally, TCP MD5 has operational limitations, including the manual management of shared keys across peers, which can become cumbersome in large-scale networks.

Recognizing the need for enhanced BGP security, the Internet community has developed several initiatives to mitigate these risks. One of the most prominent efforts is Resource Public Key Infrastructure (RPKI). RPKI provides a cryptographically secure framework for validating route origin information. By publishing Route Origin Authorizations (ROAs), IP address holders can specify which autonomous systems are authorized to originate specific prefixes. BGP routers that support RPKI validation can reject invalid route announcements, preventing many common forms of route hijacking. While RPKI adoption is growing, it is still not universally deployed, leaving significant portions of the Internet vulnerable to unvalidated routes.

BGPsec is another proposed solution aimed at securing BGP. Unlike RPKI, which focuses on origin validation, BGPsec provides cryptographic protection of the entire AS_PATH attribute, ensuring that each AS in the path has legitimately propagated the route. This prevents attackers from altering AS_PATH information to make hijacked routes appear more legitimate. However, BGPsec faces challenges related to computational overhead, complexity, and partial deployment across the Internet, making its widespread adoption a gradual process.

Beyond protocol enhancements, operational best practices are essential to securing BGP. Networks should implement strict route filtering policies, both inbound and outbound, to limit which prefixes are accepted or advertised based on known, authorized relationships.

Prefix lists, route maps, and maximum prefix limits should be used to prevent accidental or malicious route propagation. Additionally, monitoring systems should be in place to detect anomalies in BGP updates, such as unexpected changes in AS_PATHs, the appearance of new prefixes, or sudden shifts in traffic patterns.

Peering agreements and collaborative security practices between autonomous systems also play an important role in reducing BGP threats. The implementation of MANRS (Mutually Agreed Norms for Routing Security), a global initiative promoted by the Internet Society, encourages networks to adopt routing security best practices, including filtering, anti-spoofing measures, and global coordination during security incidents.

BGP security challenges will continue to evolve as the Internet grows in complexity and scale. While technical solutions such as RPKI and BGPsec offer significant improvements, the combination of protocol enhancements, strict operational controls, and industry cooperation will remain essential to safeguarding the stability and integrity of global Internet routing. As BGP continues to serve as the Internet's foundational routing protocol, addressing its security weaknesses remains a top priority for network operators, service providers, and the broader Internet community.

The Impact of BGP Hijacking

BGP hijacking is one of the most disruptive and dangerous threats to the stability and trustworthiness of the global Internet. The Border Gateway Protocol, which acts as the routing backbone for communication between autonomous systems, was not designed with security as a primary concern, leaving it susceptible to manipulation. When a BGP hijack occurs, a malicious or misconfigured network advertises IP prefixes that it does not rightfully own, diverting traffic away from its legitimate destination. The impact of such incidents is far-reaching, affecting everything from enterprise networks and cloud services to e-commerce platforms and critical infrastructure. The consequences can range from financial loss and degraded performance to privacy violations and massive service outages.

At its core, BGP hijacking undermines the basic trust model of inter-domain routing. The Internet depends on thousands of autonomous systems announcing their IP prefixes and trusting their neighbors to do the same correctly. However, when an unauthorized AS originates a prefix, it misleads other routers into sending traffic to the hijacker instead of the legitimate destination. Once traffic is redirected, the hijacker can choose to blackhole the traffic, inspect and alter data, or reroute it covertly back to the intended destination after capturing it. This last scenario, often referred to as a man-in-the-middle attack, allows the hijacker to eavesdrop on potentially sensitive information without immediately alerting users or network administrators.

The financial implications of BGP hijacking are significant. E-commerce businesses, banks, and online services can lose substantial revenue due to interrupted customer access, fraud, or data breaches caused by hijacks. For example, if a payment provider's prefixes are hijacked, users attempting to make transactions might be redirected to phishing sites or experience transaction failures. The affected business may also suffer reputational damage, customer churn, and regulatory scrutiny if the hijack results in compromised data or service downtime.

Another major consequence of BGP hijacking is the disruption of cloud services and content delivery networks. Cloud providers rely on stable BGP routing to ensure that users around the world can access resources in the nearest or most optimal data center. When a hijack redirects traffic to a rogue network or blackholes it entirely, users may experience application timeouts, degraded performance, or complete service unavailability. For organizations that depend on cloud-hosted applications or distributed edge platforms to serve their global audience, the impact of such disruptions can ripple across their entire business operations.

The impact of hijacking extends beyond private sector businesses. Governments, healthcare systems, and emergency services can also be affected. If critical infrastructure is targeted by a hijack, the resulting outages or data redirection can hinder public safety responses or compromise the confidentiality of sensitive governmental communications. There have been instances where prefixes belonging to military or research institutions were inadvertently or maliciously hijacked, creating serious national security concerns.

The cascading effect of BGP hijacking is another area of concern. Once a hijacked route is propagated through BGP, it can be accepted and further distributed by downstream autonomous systems, including major ISPs and Internet exchange points. This amplifies the scope of the hijack, causing traffic from entire regions or continents to be diverted through the malicious network. Because of the decentralized nature of BGP, where each AS makes routing decisions independently, a hijack originating from a single misconfigured router can quickly affect hundreds or thousands of networks globally.

There are also economic implications for ISPs and transit providers. Networks that accidentally propagate hijacked prefixes may find themselves handling large volumes of unintended traffic, consuming bandwidth, CPU resources, and increasing costs without any financial compensation. Moreover, their reputation may be harmed if they are perceived as contributing to routing instability. In some cases, peering agreements or customer contracts may be impacted due to traffic misdirection or service level agreement (SLA) violations caused by hijacks.

BGP hijacking also presents a unique challenge in cybersecurity. Malicious actors often use hijacking as a method to facilitate further attacks, such as DNS hijacking, phishing, or malware distribution. For instance, by hijacking a prefix that hosts DNS servers, attackers can redirect users to malicious IP addresses without altering end-user devices or local configurations. In another scenario, hijackers may impersonate legitimate websites, allowing them to capture login credentials or distribute malware under the guise of a trusted service.

For organizations, the lack of immediate visibility into BGP hijacks exacerbates the problem. Since BGP updates propagate globally in minutes and traffic rerouting happens at the network layer, end users often remain unaware of the redirection. Detection typically depends on monitoring services or third-party alerting platforms that track BGP anomalies, but these may not be deployed universally or may alert too late to prevent the initial impact. Even when detected, mitigating a hijack requires coordination between multiple autonomous systems, which may involve manual intervention, slowing down resolution times.

The human factor is another element contributing to the prevalence of BGP hijacking. Not all hijacks are deliberate acts of cyberattacks; many are the result of operational errors, such as incorrect configuration of BGP announcements or the absence of strict filtering policies. However, whether malicious or accidental, the result is often the same: large-scale traffic disruption. The Internet's vulnerability to such errors highlights the need for systemic improvements in routing security.

Despite the risks, many networks still operate without robust protections against hijacking. While initiatives like RPKI (Resource Public Key Infrastructure) offer route origin validation that can prevent the acceptance of unauthorized prefixes, adoption has been slow and uneven. Networks that fail to validate routing announcements remain vulnerable to hijacks, creating weak links in the broader Internet routing ecosystem.

Efforts to mitigate the impact of BGP hijacking also face geopolitical challenges. In some cases, hijacks originate from regions with limited regulatory oversight or differing national security priorities. This makes cross-border cooperation essential but complicated, as sovereign interests, privacy concerns, and legal frameworks vary significantly. As such, while technical solutions exist, the global nature of BGP hijacking requires a coordinated effort among governments, service providers, and technical communities to establish best practices, enforce routing security standards, and respond swiftly to incidents.

BGP hijacking serves as a reminder of the fragility of the Internet's routing infrastructure. The ease with which malicious actors or simple misconfigurations can disrupt global connectivity underscores the urgent need for better routing security practices, widespread adoption of validation technologies, and closer cooperation across the Internet community. The risks posed by hijacking affect not just technical infrastructure, but also the stability, security, and economic vitality of the digital services that underpin modern society.

BGP Monitoring and Logging

The Border Gateway Protocol is the central nervous system of the Internet, enabling autonomous systems to exchange reachability information across the globe. Given BGP's critical role in ensuring Internet stability and routing efficiency, monitoring and logging of BGP sessions and updates are indispensable components of responsible network operations. Without proper visibility into BGP's behavior, network operators cannot effectively detect routing anomalies, troubleshoot connectivity issues, or prevent security threats such as route hijacking or route leaks. BGP monitoring and logging provide the data necessary to maintain control over routing decisions and ensure the ongoing health of an autonomous system's connectivity to the broader Internet.

At its core, BGP monitoring focuses on observing the health and state of BGP sessions established between routers. This includes tracking the status of both internal BGP (iBGP) and external BGP (eBGP) peerings. Network operators must have insight into session establishment, keepalive exchanges, and session terminations to understand the stability of their BGP relationships. Alerts for session flaps, long-lasting session drops, or frequent restarts are vital, as these events may signal underlying physical connectivity issues, misconfigurations, or even denial-of-service attacks targeting the TCP port used by BGP.

Logging BGP session events is the first layer of this monitoring strategy. Routers generate logs for critical session states, including transitions between idle, active, established, and closing phases of the BGP finite state machine. These logs are often forwarded to centralized syslog servers for long-term storage and analysis. By examining historical logs, network engineers can identify recurring instability patterns, such as repeated session resets at the same time each day, which might point to faulty equipment or network congestion.

In addition to session monitoring, BGP route update logging plays a crucial role in understanding the dynamics of route advertisements and withdrawals. BGP routers continuously exchange UPDATE messages containing new prefixes, withdrawn routes, or attribute changes. Monitoring the rate and frequency of these updates is critical for maintaining routing table stability. For example, a sudden surge in route advertisements could indicate a misconfigured peer advertising thousands of unnecessary prefixes, while excessive route flaps could suggest instability in the remote network or improper route dampening settings.

To capture these events, most routers offer BGP debug logging, which records detailed information about UPDATE messages. While debug logging is typically used selectively due to its potential to impact router performance, it is an essential tool for diagnosing specific routing problems, such as incorrect AS_PATH attributes, unexpected next-hop values, or improperly tagged communities. Debug logs provide packet-level visibility into BGP communication, allowing engineers to trace how and why certain routes are selected, rejected, or withdrawn from the routing table.

However, the volume and complexity of BGP logs can quickly overwhelm manual analysis efforts, particularly in large networks with dozens or hundreds of peers. To address this, organizations rely on specialized BGP monitoring platforms that automate the collection and analysis of routing data. These platforms connect to routers using BGP monitoring protocols such as BGP Monitoring Protocol (BMP) or SNMP and collect real-time data about session status, prefix counts, and routing anomalies.

BMP, for example, provides a standardized way for routers to send unaltered BGP routing information to external collectors. Unlike traditional route monitoring via BGP peering, BMP sessions do not participate in the BGP decision process and do not influence routing decisions. This makes BMP an ideal mechanism for passive observation of BGP activity without introducing additional routing complexity. BMP collectors aggregate this data and often integrate with network telemetry systems, providing dashboards and alerts for anomalies such as sudden increases in prefix withdrawals, unexpected AS_PATH changes, or unanticipated next-hop modifications.

Another powerful BGP monitoring method is the use of route collectors and looking glasses. Many networks participate in global route collection projects such as RIPE RIS or RouteViews, which gather routing information from thousands of networks and make it publicly available for research and operational use. These route collectors act as passive BGP peers, receiving updates from participating autonomous systems and providing an external perspective on how routes are propagated across the Internet. By comparing a network's local routing table with global collector data, operators can detect inconsistencies, leaks, or hijacks that may not be immediately visible within their own network.

Looking glass servers provide another external view of routing behavior, offering a way to query routers from geographically diverse locations to verify route visibility and path selection. Many service providers and Internet exchanges operate public looking glass services, allowing engineers to check whether specific prefixes are reachable and to inspect BGP attributes from different vantage points. This can be invaluable for diagnosing issues such as asymmetric routing, missing advertisements, or unexpected route filtering by upstream providers.

In addition to route-level monitoring, modern BGP monitoring systems often incorporate analytics to detect patterns indicative of security threats. For example, route hijacking incidents frequently involve sudden announcements of more-specific prefixes, unauthorized origin AS numbers, or unexpected changes in AS_PATHs. Monitoring platforms can automatically flag these anomalies, providing real-time alerts to network operators who can then take corrective action, such as filtering the hijacked routes or coordinating with upstream providers to contain the issue.

Advanced BGP monitoring systems also offer historical route visualization, enabling operators to trace routing events over days, weeks, or months. This feature is essential for understanding how routing changes evolve over time, evaluating the impact of network upgrades or policy changes, and preparing reports for stakeholders or regulatory bodies following significant routing incidents.

Beyond security and troubleshooting, BGP monitoring and logging are key tools for performance optimization and capacity planning. By analyzing trends in prefix counts, route churn, and session stability, operators can anticipate the need for router upgrades, peer reconfigurations, or changes in traffic engineering policies. For instance, a gradual increase in the number of received prefixes from a particular peer might signal growth in the peer's network, prompting a review of maximum prefix limits or route filtering rules.

The effectiveness of BGP monitoring is ultimately dependent on the ability to act on the insights gained. Network operators must integrate BGP monitoring with their operational workflows, incorporating alerts into network operations centers (NOCs) and automating responses to common issues. For example, automated scripts may temporarily dampen flapping routes or initiate BGP session resets when persistent instability is detected.

BGP monitoring and logging are critical for maintaining the health, security, and resilience of modern networks. They provide the visibility required to detect routing anomalies, safeguard against threats, and ensure optimal routing decisions. As the Internet continues to grow and routing dynamics become more complex, robust BGP monitoring strategies will remain a cornerstone of operational excellence and network stability.

BGP Best Practices

The Border Gateway Protocol serves as the foundation of inter-domain routing, connecting thousands of autonomous systems worldwide. As the Internet has grown in complexity and scale, adhering to best practices for BGP configuration and management has become essential to ensure stability, security, and optimal performance. Best practices for BGP cover several key areas, including route filtering, security hardening, redundancy, traffic engineering, and monitoring. Following these principles helps network operators maintain a robust and resilient BGP deployment while protecting both their own networks and the wider Internet community from disruptions and threats.

A fundamental best practice for BGP is implementing strict route filtering on both inbound and outbound advertisements. Networks should only accept prefixes from peers that are explicitly authorized and verified. Inbound route filters should validate that routes received from customers, peers, or upstream providers match the expected prefixes registered in Internet Routing Registries (IRRs) or as defined in business agreements. Outbound filters are equally critical and should prevent the accidental advertisement of internal-only prefixes, private IP address space, or customer-specific routes to unauthorized external peers. Comprehensive filtering reduces the risk of route leaks and accidental propagation of incorrect routing information to the global Internet.

Another key best practice is the use of prefix limits on BGP sessions. Configuring maximum prefix thresholds for each BGP neighbor helps prevent a misconfigured or malicious peer from overwhelming the router with an excessive number of route advertisements. If the number of prefixes received exceeds the defined limit, the router can shut down the session or trigger an alert to operators, mitigating potential memory exhaustion or CPU overload. Adjusting these limits according to each peer's expected prefix count is essential for protecting network infrastructure.

Authentication of BGP sessions is also a critical step in hardening BGP against session hijacking and spoofed updates. Operators should configure TCP MD5 authentication or, where available, TCP-AO (TCP Authentication Option) on all external BGP sessions. By exchanging a shared secret between peers, routers can verify that BGP updates are coming from a legitimate source, reducing the likelihood of malicious actors injecting unauthorized routes into the session. Although this does not secure the BGP protocol itself against all threats, it prevents unauthorized peers from establishing sessions with the router.

Deployment of route origin validation mechanisms, such as Resource Public Key Infrastructure (RPKI), is an increasingly important best practice. RPKI enables networks to cryptographically verify whether a BGP route originates from the autonomous system authorized to announce it. By rejecting invalid routes and favoring valid ones, RPKI implementation significantly reduces the risk of route hijacking and unintentional prefix misannouncement. Networks should regularly update their RPKI validators and incorporate origin validation into their BGP routing policies.

Ensuring redundancy and high availability is another essential BGP best practice. Autonomous systems should establish redundant BGP sessions with multiple upstream providers, peers, or route reflectors to avoid single points of failure. By implementing multi-homed designs and maintaining diverse physical paths to upstream networks, operators can minimize the risk of outages caused by equipment failures, link disruptions, or upstream incidents. Load balancing traffic across redundant BGP sessions and using attributes such as LOCAL_PREF and AS_PATH prepending enables fine-grained traffic engineering while maintaining failover capabilities.

Proper configuration of BGP attributes is critical for maintaining control over routing behavior. Networks should standardize their use of attributes such as LOCAL_PREF, MED, and BGP communities to influence path selection in accordance with traffic engineering goals. For example, increasing the LOCAL_PREF on preferred outbound routes ensures that traffic exits the network via the most desirable provider or peer, while BGP communities can be used to automate routing decisions across larger networks or coordinate routing behavior with upstream providers.

Maintaining a clean and organized routing policy is also recommended. Operators should document their routing policies and apply consistent naming conventions to route maps, prefix lists, and community tags. This improves maintainability and reduces the likelihood of misconfiguration during network changes or when onboarding new peers or customers. Regular audits of BGP configurations and policies help identify outdated or redundant entries that may conflict with current routing objectives.

Monitoring and logging form another pillar of BGP best practices. Operators should deploy comprehensive BGP monitoring systems that track session status, prefix counts, route changes, and anomalous behavior. Implementing real-time alerts for session flaps, unexpected prefix changes, or invalid RPKI validations allows for rapid incident response. Additionally, historical log analysis helps diagnose recurring issues and improves understanding of long-term routing patterns and trends.

Participation in global route collection initiatives, such as RIPE RIS or RouteViews, allows network operators to gain visibility into how their prefixes are propagated across the Internet. Utilizing public looking glass services or deploying private looking glass servers within their own networks enables engineers to verify route visibility and investigate path selection from multiple perspectives. These tools enhance situational awareness and assist in troubleshooting routing issues or verifying traffic engineering configurations.

A proactive approach to network security further complements BGP best practices. Operators should filter bogon prefixes (unallocated or reserved IP space) and implement ingress and egress filtering to prevent IP address spoofing. Anti-spoofing measures, such as Unicast Reverse Path Forwarding (uRPF), help protect against IP address spoofing attacks that could be used in combination with BGP hijacking or other routing-based exploits.

Staying informed about evolving routing security standards and collaborating with the Internet community is also recommended. Participation in initiatives such as MANRS (Mutually Agreed Norms for Routing Security) demonstrates a commitment to responsible routing practices and contributes to the collective security of the Internet. MANRS provides actionable guidelines, including the implementation of filtering, anti-spoofing, coordination, and validation mechanisms that align with industry-recognized BGP best practices.

Finally, network operators should develop and regularly test incident response plans specific to BGP events. These plans should outline procedures for identifying and mitigating route leaks, hijacks, or session failures, as well as communication protocols for notifying upstream providers, peers, or affected customers. Rapid containment and resolution of BGP-related incidents are vital for preserving network stability and protecting customer trust.

Incorporating BGP best practices into day-to-day network operations is essential for maintaining a secure, stable, and well-performing routing environment. As BGP continues to power the global Internet and support modern services such as cloud computing, content delivery, and enterprise connectivity, following these principles becomes increasingly important. Through a combination of sound technical configurations, proactive security measures, and effective operational workflows, network operators can ensure that their BGP implementations meet the demands of today's complex and interconnected digital landscape.

BGP Troubleshooting Techniques

Troubleshooting BGP issues is one of the most important and complex tasks in network operations. As the protocol that governs inter-domain routing across the global Internet and within large enterprises, BGP plays a crucial role in ensuring reachability, stability, and performance. However, the distributed nature of BGP, combined with its policy-driven decision-making process, means that diagnosing routing anomalies, session instability, or traffic engineering problems often requires deep technical knowledge and a systematic approach. Effective troubleshooting techniques involve analyzing BGP session health, inspecting routing tables, verifying BGP attributes, reviewing filtering policies, and leveraging a range of diagnostic tools to identify and resolve issues.

A common starting point for BGP troubleshooting is verifying the status of BGP sessions. If two routers fail to establish or maintain a BGP session, traffic between their respective autonomous systems will not flow as expected. Operators should begin by checking whether the BGP session is in an established state. If the session remains stuck in idle, active, or connect states, the cause may be related to TCP connectivity issues, incorrect IP addresses, or access control lists blocking TCP port 179. Verifying that both routers can reach each other at the transport layer using tools like ping or traceroute is essential to rule out basic network connectivity issues. Additionally, reviewing firewall rules and ensuring that TCP port 179 is open is a critical step.

Once basic connectivity is confirmed, misconfigured BGP peer settings often come under scrutiny. Common configuration errors include mismatched AS numbers, incorrect neighbor IP addresses, or failure to configure proper BGP authentication. If TCP MD5 or TCP-AO authentication is used, both peers must share the same password. Any inconsistency in these values will prevent the BGP session from establishing. Logs from the router's syslog or debug output can provide valuable clues, often showing errors like MD5 checksum mismatch or passive session timeouts.

For established BGP sessions that still exhibit problems, attention turns to the routes being exchanged. If expected prefixes are not received from a neighbor, operators should verify inbound route filters. Prefix lists, route maps, and policy statements may unintentionally block or modify routes, preventing them from being installed in the local BGP table. Reviewing filter configurations and comparing them against documented routing policies helps ensure that the correct prefixes are being accepted. On the sending side, outbound filters should be checked to confirm that the local router is advertising the correct prefixes to its neighbors.

Inspecting BGP attributes is another key troubleshooting technique. If multiple routes to the same destination exist but the router is not selecting the expected path, analyzing BGP attributes such as weight, LOCAL_PREF, AS_PATH, MED, and origin code will help reveal why. For instance, if a route with a lower AS_PATH length is available but the router chooses a longer path, a higher LOCAL_PREF value or weight on the longer path might be overriding the usual path selection logic. Displaying detailed BGP route information using commands like show ip bgp <prefix> or equivalent on the device will reveal the full attribute set for each route, providing insight into the decision-making process.

Route dampening and flap detection mechanisms may also impact routing behavior. BGP routers use dampening to suppress unstable routes that frequently appear and disappear, preventing them from contributing to routing churn. However, overly aggressive dampening thresholds may suppress legitimate prefixes for extended periods. By reviewing dampening logs and the route's penalty values, operators can determine if a route has been suppressed due to flapping and adjust the dampening configuration if necessary.

Session stability issues, such as frequent BGP flaps, often require a closer look at underlying network conditions. Packet loss, high latency, or unstable physical links can cause session resets, especially in long-haul or congested networks. Examining interface statistics on both routers for signs of errors, collisions, or dropped packets can pinpoint physical or Layer 2 problems affecting BGP. Additionally, reviewing CPU and memory usage on routers may reveal resource exhaustion impacting BGP session maintenance.

Another critical area of BGP troubleshooting is next-hop reachability. BGP relies on the underlying IGP to resolve next-hop addresses for routes learned from eBGP neighbors. If the next-hop IP is unreachable or not present in the IGP's routing table, the BGP route will be considered invalid and will not be installed. Operators should verify that next-hop addresses are reachable and correctly redistributed into the IGP. The use of the next-hop-self command in BGP configurations can also address next-hop reachability issues in iBGP environments by ensuring that local routers set themselves as the next hop when redistributing eBGP-learned routes internally.

External tools and services are invaluable during BGP troubleshooting, especially when dealing with Internet-wide anomalies. Public looking glass servers provide a global perspective on how routes are seen by other autonomous systems, helping to identify if a prefix is being propagated as expected. Similarly, route collectors such as RIPE RIS or RouteViews allow operators to inspect historical and real-time routing data from multiple vantage points. These insights can reveal route leaks, hijacks, or propagation inconsistencies that may not be visible within the local AS.

BGP Monitoring Protocol (BMP) collectors and other telemetry platforms can also assist by providing real-time visibility into BGP updates and session events. These tools can flag sudden changes in prefix counts, unexpected AS_PATH alterations, or shifts in next-hop information, enabling proactive identification of issues before they escalate into major outages.

Troubleshooting BGP also involves collaboration with peers and upstream providers. When issues extend beyond the local network, such as missing prefixes or unexpected traffic paths, coordinating with neighboring AS operators can uncover misconfigurations or policy mismatches on their side. For example, if a transit provider accidentally applies restrictive filters or incorrectly prepends AS_PATHs, it can affect how other networks reach your prefixes.

Maintaining clear communication channels with external peers accelerates problem resolution.

Finally, maintaining comprehensive documentation and adhering to change management procedures greatly facilitates troubleshooting efforts. When BGP anomalies occur, having accurate records of existing policies, session configurations, and recent changes allows operators to systematically rule out potential causes. Change logs help identify whether recent adjustments to routing policies, filter lists, or infrastructure might be contributing factors.

BGP troubleshooting requires a blend of analytical thinking, deep protocol knowledge, and operational discipline. By following a structured methodology that examines session states, routing policies, attribute behaviors, and network health, engineers can effectively diagnose and resolve even the most complex BGP issues. In modern networks where BGP underpins critical services, timely and accurate troubleshooting ensures business continuity, service quality, and the overall integrity of Internet routing.

Case Studies of BGP Incidents

Over the years, the Border Gateway Protocol has been at the center of numerous high-profile network disruptions and security incidents that have affected Internet services on a global scale. Each incident highlights the critical role BGP plays in the interconnected fabric of the Internet and demonstrates how vulnerabilities or misconfigurations can lead to massive outages, traffic rerouting, or even the compromise of sensitive data. By studying these real-world cases, network operators and engineers can better understand the consequences of BGP mishandling and the importance of implementing strong routing policies and security controls.

One of the most well-known and widely discussed BGP incidents occurred in April 2010 when a Chinese ISP, China Telecom, unintentionally announced around 37,000 prefixes that belonged to other networks, including routes from the United States Department of Defense, major financial institutions, and global Internet service providers. This incident, often described as a massive BGP hijack, resulted in traffic from various regions being rerouted through China Telecom's network for approximately 18 minutes. While there was no public evidence of malicious intent or traffic manipulation, the incident demonstrated how a single incorrect advertisement could attract traffic from across the globe. The ripple effects were felt worldwide, raising concerns about the fragility of BGP and the potential for similar events to be exploited for surveillance or cyberattacks.

Another significant BGP event took place in February 2008 when Pakistan Telecom inadvertently hijacked YouTube's IP address space. In an attempt to block access to YouTube within Pakistan, the telecom provider used BGP to advertise a more specific prefix for YouTube's IP space, redirecting traffic bound for YouTube to a null route inside Pakistan. Unfortunately, this route leak was propagated to the global Internet by Pakistan Telecom's upstream provider, PCCW, a major international carrier. As a result, traffic from users around the world attempting to reach YouTube was blackholed. YouTube became unreachable globally for several hours until corrective actions were taken. This incident became a textbook example of how route filtering failures at upstream providers can lead to widespread outages.

In April 2020, another BGP hijack incident caused disruptions in global traffic patterns when Russian telecommunications provider Rostelecom began announcing prefixes belonging to more than 30 large networks, including major cloud providers such as Google, Amazon, and Akamai. The hijack lasted for several hours and led to the redirection of traffic intended for these networks through Russia. The incident triggered renewed discussions on the importance of deploying RPKI and filtering policies to prevent the propagation of unauthorized BGP advertisements. Many observers speculated on the geopolitical and security implications of such hijacks, as traffic passing through a foreign AS could be subjected to surveillance or other forms of interception.

A different type of BGP-related disruption occurred in June 2019 when Cloudflare and other services experienced significant downtime due to a route leak originating from Swiss ISP Safe Host. A misconfiguration by a small customer network caused thousands of Cloudflare prefixes to be advertised with an unintended AS_PATH, sending traffic through a transit provider that did not have the capacity to handle the massive influx of traffic. The resulting congestion affected Cloudflare's services, leading to slowdowns and outages for websites relying on Cloudflare's CDN and DDoS protection services. This event highlighted the issue of traffic asymmetry and how unintentional routing changes can overload parts of the Internet that are not dimensioned to handle transit-level traffic.

In 2014, a critical BGP mishap affected large swaths of the Internet when a Brazilian ISP mistakenly announced a full table of Internet routes (about 500,000 prefixes) as being part of its own prefix space. This triggered widespread instability and route churn across multiple networks, especially in South America. The announcement was rapidly propagated through several Tier 1 providers, leading to degraded service for end users, dropped traffic, and increased CPU loads on routers globally as they processed the flurry of updates and withdrawals. This event underscored the risks posed by misconfigured aggregation policies and the need for more stringent prefix filtering, particularly on the edges of smaller networks.

Even large technology companies are not immune to BGP-related problems. In November 2018, Google Cloud services were impacted when MainOne, a provider based in Nigeria, announced Google IP prefixes with a more specific AS_PATH. The misrouted traffic traversed China Telecom and other networks before eventually being dropped or degraded. The hijack affected traffic destined for Google's business-critical services such as G Suite and Google Cloud Platform, disrupting services for thousands of enterprise customers. The combination of routing through non-optimal paths and packet loss further highlighted how the interconnectedness of the global routing system makes all networks, regardless of size or sophistication, vulnerable to improper route advertisements from other networks.

Beyond hijacks and leaks, operational BGP incidents often involve session flaps or misconfigured traffic engineering. In 2015, a major North American carrier experienced repeated BGP session resets across its backbone after deploying a faulty software update on core routers. The session instability triggered route churn, forcing routers to repeatedly recalculate best paths and causing transient outages and slowdowns for customers. The event emphasized how software issues and mismanaged router upgrades can introduce BGP instability even within highly redundant and well-designed networks.

Another dimension to BGP incidents is the exploitation of hijacks to enable more sophisticated attacks. In 2017, security researchers discovered that BGP hijacks were being used to redirect traffic from cryptocurrency mining pools and siphon off mining rewards. In these cases, attackers would hijack IP prefixes of mining pools to redirect the mining traffic to servers under their control. This example demonstrates how BGP hijacking can be used for financially motivated attacks and shows that the threat landscape is not limited to large-scale outages but extends to more targeted, stealthy forms of exploitation.

Each of these incidents reveals a common theme: the global routing system remains highly susceptible to misconfiguration, human error, and malicious exploitation due to BGP's trust-based model and lack of built-in security. While technical solutions such as RPKI, BGPsec, and MANRS-compliant filtering practices can reduce the likelihood of these events, the reliance on voluntary cooperation and fragmented deployment leaves gaps in the Internet's defenses.

Studying these real-world BGP incidents provides invaluable lessons on the critical need for filtering, route validation, proactive monitoring, and collaborative response between network operators. It also reinforces the importance of automation and modern network tools to catch anomalies before they propagate widely. In a world where organizations rely on the Internet for everything from business transactions to critical infrastructure operations, each BGP failure or hijack serves as a reminder of the urgent need to enhance routing security and resilience at all levels.

BGP and Internet Exchange Points

The Border Gateway Protocol plays a pivotal role in the operation and efficiency of Internet Exchange Points, commonly known as IXPs. As physical infrastructures where networks, also referred to as autonomous systems, meet to exchange traffic directly, IXPs are a fundamental part of the global Internet ecosystem. They enable multiple networks to interconnect at a single location, reducing the reliance on upstream transit providers and allowing for more efficient and cost-effective routing of data. BGP is the protocol that facilitates this interconnection, making IXPs hubs of inter-domain routing activity that rely on the precise and stable operation of BGP sessions between participants.

At the heart of every IXP is a layer 2 Ethernet switch or switching fabric to which all participating networks physically connect. Each participant in an IXP establishes BGP sessions with other participants to exchange routing information directly. This process is called peering, and it allows networks to send traffic directly to one another without the need for intermediate transit providers. By leveraging BGP sessions at IXPs, networks can bypass more expensive or longer Internet routes, improving performance, reducing latency, and lowering operational costs.

BGP at an IXP typically involves two types of peering relationships: bilateral and multilateral peering. In bilateral peering, two networks establish a direct BGP session with each other. This approach gives each network complete control over who they peer with and allows for more customized routing policies. However, in IXPs with hundreds of participants, establishing and maintaining bilateral sessions with every potential peer becomes operationally challenging. To address this, many IXPs offer a route server, which facilitates multilateral peering.

The route server acts as a centralized BGP-speaking system that allows networks to establish a single BGP session with the route server rather than multiple bilateral sessions with each individual peer. The route server collects and distributes routing information between all participating networks, streamlining the peering process and significantly reducing the administrative overhead. Despite this convenience, it is important to note that the route server only relays BGP updates and does not participate in the data forwarding path. Traffic still flows directly between the peering networks over the IXP's switching fabric.

When establishing BGP sessions at an IXP, each autonomous system announces the prefixes it wants to make reachable to other participants. Networks use BGP attributes such as AS_PATH, MED, and BGP communities to influence how peers select routes. For example, by setting BGP community values, networks can instruct the route server to limit the advertisement of certain prefixes to specific peers, providing fine-grained control over routing decisions even in a multilateral peering environment.

The benefits of participating in an IXP extend beyond just performance improvements. By connecting to an IXP and using BGP to peer with multiple networks, operators can improve the resilience and redundancy of their routing infrastructure. If one upstream provider or transit path fails, traffic can continue to flow through direct peering relationships established at the IXP. This diversity enhances network reliability and provides additional options for traffic engineering.

From a security standpoint, BGP at IXPs must be carefully managed to prevent common threats such as route leaks or prefix hijacking. IXPs typically enforce best practices and technical policies to help safeguard participants. These may include requiring participants to filter bogon prefixes, validating AS numbers, and using strict prefix filtering to ensure that only authorized prefixes are advertised. Additionally, many route servers at IXPs now support RPKI-based origin validation, which helps prevent the propagation of invalid or hijacked routes.

Monitoring and troubleshooting BGP sessions at IXPs is essential for maintaining a stable peering environment. Operators often use BGP session monitoring tools to track session health, prefix counts, and routing anomalies. IXPs frequently provide participants with access to route server looking glass services, which allow networks to view routing tables from the perspective of the route server and verify how their prefixes are being advertised to other participants.

Another important aspect of BGP at IXPs is traffic optimization. By establishing BGP peerings with networks that exchange large volumes of traffic, such as content delivery networks, cloud providers, or regional ISPs, networks can keep more traffic local to the region. This reduces the need for transiting traffic through upstream providers located in distant geographic regions, improving latency and reducing operational expenses related to upstream transit costs. For content providers and large enterprises, peering at multiple IXPs globally also helps bring their content closer to end users, enhancing the overall user experience.

The evolution of BGP and IXPs has also enabled more sophisticated service offerings. For example, many IXPs offer private interconnection services known as private VLANs or cross-connects, allowing two participants to set up private BGP peerings within the IXP infrastructure without traversing the public peering LAN. This can be used for dedicated services, private peering agreements, or specialized traffic engineering scenarios where greater control over traffic flows is desired.

BGP at IXPs is also central to the functioning of regional and national Internet ecosystems. In many developing markets, the establishment of a local IXP combined with proper BGP peering policies has helped reduce international bandwidth costs by keeping local traffic within the country or region. This localization of traffic promotes the growth of local digital economies, accelerates Internet access, and decreases the dependency on expensive international transit links.

Some of the largest IXPs in the world, such as DE-CIX in Frankfurt, AMS-IX in Amsterdam, and LINX in London, operate route servers that manage tens of thousands of BGP sessions and exchange hundreds of gigabits per second of traffic. These IXPs serve as vital peering points for global cloud providers, streaming services, Tier 1 ISPs, and enterprises alike. The role of BGP in orchestrating these complex, high-capacity interconnections is indispensable.

Ultimately, the synergy between BGP and IXPs exemplifies the collaborative and decentralized nature of the Internet. By leveraging BGP to manage peering relationships at IXPs, networks gain better performance, greater control over routing policies, and improved resilience, all while reducing costs. The operational success of IXPs hinges on the correct and secure implementation of BGP sessions, proper filtering, and continuous monitoring to ensure that Internet traffic flows smoothly and securely between autonomous systems around the world.

Understanding BGP Flap Dampening

BGP flap dampening is a mechanism designed to improve the stability of the Internet's routing infrastructure by minimizing the negative effects of route flapping. Route flapping occurs when a network prefix is repeatedly advertised and withdrawn in a short period of time, causing instability and unnecessary churn in global routing tables. Every time a prefix flaps, routers must process the updates, recalculate their routing decisions, and propagate changes to neighboring autonomous systems. In large-scale networks, excessive flapping can consume significant CPU and memory resources on routers and contribute to routing convergence delays. BGP flap dampening helps mitigate this issue by penalizing unstable prefixes and suppressing them until their stability improves.

The core concept behind BGP flap dampening is to assign a penalty value to a prefix each time it flaps. When a prefix's accumulated penalty exceeds a predefined suppress threshold, the route is suppressed, meaning it is withdrawn and not advertised to other peers. This prevents the unstable prefix from continuously impacting routing tables across the Internet. Over time, the penalty value decays according to a configured half-life, and once it drops below a reuse threshold, the prefix is unsuppressed and reintroduced into the routing table. This damping mechanism effectively isolates instability, allowing networks to focus processing resources on more stable prefixes.

The introduction of flap dampening addressed a growing concern during the rapid expansion of the Internet, especially as the size of the global BGP table increased. As more autonomous systems came online and more prefixes were advertised, the potential for instability grew, leading operators to seek mechanisms to reduce unnecessary route propagation and stabilize the routing environment. Flap dampening became a widely adopted solution, particularly among large service providers and Tier 1 ISPs, where the volume of route updates from various customers and peers could become overwhelming during periods of instability.

To configure flap dampening effectively, network operators must tune four key parameters: the penalty value assigned to each flap, the suppress threshold, the reuse threshold, and the half-life timer. The penalty value defines how severe each flap is treated. A typical penalty might be 1000 points per flap. The suppress threshold, often set around 2000 or 3000 points, determines when a route will be suppressed. The reuse threshold, commonly lower than the suppress threshold, defines the point at which the route will be eligible for re-advertisement. The half-life determines how quickly the penalty decays over time, typically measured in minutes. By carefully adjusting these parameters, network operators can strike a balance between preventing instability and avoiding the unnecessary suppression of critical prefixes.

While flap dampening can greatly reduce routing churn, its implementation must be approached with caution. Overly aggressive dampening settings can lead to the unintended suppression of legitimate prefixes that experience transient instability due to link flaps or maintenance windows. For example, a critical service provider prefix might flap several times due to fiber cuts or hardware maintenance, and if flap dampening thresholds are too low, the prefix could be suppressed from the global routing table, effectively causing a blackhole for all traffic destined to that network. For this reason, best practices recommend applying flap dampening selectively, targeting only customer or peer routes prone to instability rather than applying it globally to all prefixes.

Some operators have taken an even more conservative approach by avoiding flap dampening on critical infrastructure routes or prefixes originated by Tier 1 providers, given that these routes are essential for maintaining Internet connectivity. Instead, flap dampening is commonly reserved for edge networks or customer prefixes with a history of flapping. Another common strategy is to adjust the threshold values to make the suppress threshold high enough that only the most unstable prefixes are suppressed, while more stable prefixes that experience occasional flaps remain unaffected.

From a technical perspective, flap dampening is implemented at the routing policy level on BGP-speaking routers. Modern router operating systems provide commands to enable dampening globally, per peer, or per prefix, giving network engineers granular control over how and where dampening is applied. Monitoring dampened routes is also an essential part of managing this feature, as operators must be aware of which prefixes are currently suppressed and when they are expected to re-enter the routing table. Logs and show commands typically display the accumulated penalty values, suppress/reuse thresholds, and the time remaining before the penalty decays below the reuse threshold.

Flap dampening interacts with other routing stability mechanisms, such as BGP route flap detection (RFD) and maximum prefix limits. While flap dampening focuses on suppressing unstable prefixes, RFD provides alerts or counters to help operators identify chronic flapping issues at the source. In addition, maximum prefix limits serve as a safeguard to prevent routers from accepting more prefixes than expected from a peer, providing an additional layer of protection against routing table overload.

In recent years, some operators and research communities have debated the continued use of flap dampening in modern networks. Improvements in router hardware, faster CPUs, and more sophisticated control planes have made routing devices more resilient to churn. As a result, certain operators have relaxed flap dampening policies or removed them entirely in favor of monitoring and addressing flapping events through operational processes. However, flap dampening still plays an important role in networks where router resources are limited, or where specific customers or peers have a history of causing instability through route flaps.

Another consideration in modern deployments is the role of RPKI and route validation frameworks. By rejecting invalid or hijacked routes through origin validation before they can propagate, RPKI complements flap dampening by reducing the likelihood of rogue prefixes causing instability. Combined with strict inbound route filtering and prefix-lists, flap dampening remains a valuable tool in a broader routing security and stability strategy.

Ultimately, BGP flap dampening offers a practical mechanism to mitigate the effects of routing instability caused by frequent flapping. While it requires careful tuning and operational oversight, when used correctly, it contributes to a more stable and predictable Internet routing environment. As networks continue to grow in size and complexity, flap dampening provides network engineers with one more lever to preserve routing table stability and ensure that the

Internet remains resilient even in the face of localized disruptions or misconfigurations.

Graceful Restart and BGP

Graceful Restart is a key enhancement to the Border Gateway Protocol that addresses one of the most common operational challenges in routing: session interruptions caused by planned or unplanned router reboots or control plane failures. Traditionally, when a BGP session resets due to a router reload or software failure, all routes learned from that peer are withdrawn immediately. This triggers route recalculations and potentially network-wide churn, where routers must recompute best paths and re-converge. In large networks, such instability can lead to packet loss, degraded performance, and customer-visible outages. Graceful Restart was developed to minimize these impacts by allowing BGP sessions to recover quickly without causing unnecessary route withdrawals and route flapping.

Graceful Restart works by maintaining forwarding state on the data plane during a control plane disruption. In other words, when a router supporting Graceful Restart experiences a control plane failure or is intentionally rebooted, its BGP peers will continue to forward traffic to it as long as its data plane, or forwarding plane, remains operational. This is achieved by temporarily preserving BGP routes that would otherwise be withdrawn during the session reset. The restarting router then has a period, known as the Graceful Restart timer, to re-establish the BGP session and synchronize its routing information with its peer before normal BGP behavior resumes.

The mechanism relies on both routers in the BGP session supporting Graceful Restart capabilities. The feature is negotiated between peers using BGP capability negotiation during the session establishment process. If both routers agree to support Graceful Restart, they mark their capability in the BGP OPEN message exchange. Once the capability is established, the routers will treat subsequent control plane restarts differently, preserving routing information and suppressing route withdrawals during the restart period.

A common scenario where Graceful Restart provides value is during planned maintenance, such as router upgrades or software patches. In many networks, upgrades require control plane processes to restart or the router to reboot, disrupting BGP sessions temporarily. Without Graceful Restart, this disruption would trigger route withdrawals across all downstream routers, leading to routing reconvergence and potential traffic blackholing as paths are recalculated. With Graceful Restart, the peers retain the routes learned from the restarting router and continue forwarding packets as normal, preventing unnecessary instability.

During the restart process, the peer router marks the session as "in Graceful Restart state" and starts the Graceful Restart timer. This timer typically ranges from 60 to 180 seconds but can be adjusted according to network requirements. The restarting router is expected to bring its control plane back online, re-establish the BGP session, and re-advertise all valid routes before the timer expires. If the restart is successful, normal BGP operations resume without route withdrawals. If the timer expires before the restarting router re-establishes the session, the peer will then withdraw the previously preserved routes and trigger a typical BGP reconvergence process.

While Graceful Restart is highly effective in reducing disruption, it introduces some operational considerations. One such consideration is that during the Graceful Restart period, the restarting router's routes are considered "stale" by its peers. This means that although they are retained for forwarding purposes, they may not reflect the most accurate or updated state of the network. To mitigate this, peers often mark these routes as "stale" in the routing table but continue to use them until they are refreshed or invalidated based on the timer's expiration.

Another important aspect of Graceful Restart is the Forwarding State bit included in the BGP GR capability advertisement. This bit indicates whether the restarting router is capable of maintaining its forwarding state while the control plane restarts. If the forwarding plane is functional, the peer will trust that packets are still being forwarded correctly to their destinations. However, if the router's data plane also fails or if the forwarding state bit is not set, the peer will treat the router as completely unavailable and revert to normal BGP behavior, withdrawing the routes immediately.

Graceful Restart is commonly used in conjunction with Non-Stop Forwarding (NSF), a related concept implemented by router vendors to ensure that the forwarding plane continues to operate even during control plane failures. NSF preserves hardware-based forwarding entries, such as those installed in the router's forwarding information base (FIB), to maintain traffic flows. Graceful Restart works at the BGP protocol level, while NSF functions at the platform level, ensuring seamless continuity during both hardware and software disruptions.

For networks with multiple upstream providers or diverse peering relationships, Graceful Restart can provide significant performance and stability benefits. By suppressing route flaps during transient control plane failures or planned maintenance windows, it reduces the workload on routers and speeds up the recovery process. This is particularly valuable for large service providers and data center operators who manage thousands of prefixes and cannot afford the risks associated with widespread route churn.

However, careful planning is needed when implementing Graceful Restart. If not configured properly, or if network policies do not take it into account, operators may inadvertently preserve stale routes longer than intended, creating potential inconsistencies in traffic paths. For example, if a critical link fails during the Graceful Restart period and the restarting router has no visibility of the failure due to its downed control plane, traffic may continue to flow into a blackhole.

Another consideration is that Graceful Restart only solves part of the routing disruption challenge. In scenarios involving multiple protocols, such as when BGP runs in parallel with OSPF, IS-IS, or MPLS label distribution protocols, the success of a graceful recovery depends on the consistent and coordinated behavior of all protocols. Some implementations extend graceful restart-like mechanisms to other protocols, such as OSPF Graceful Restart or IS-IS Restart Signaling, to ensure that link-state databases and label-switched paths (LSPs) are also preserved.

Operators must also monitor BGP session logs and diagnostic outputs to ensure that Graceful Restart is functioning as intended. Events such as "peer in restart mode" or "routes marked as stale" should trigger additional validation steps by network engineers to confirm that traffic is indeed flowing as expected and that forwarding entries are not being misapplied. Network automation platforms and monitoring tools that support Graceful Restart-aware alerts are helpful in this regard, providing real-time visibility into the state of the routing plane during control plane disruptions.

Graceful Restart has become an essential feature in modern IP and MPLS networks, where uptime and service continuity are critical. By reducing the operational impact of router failures or reboots, Graceful Restart contributes to improved customer experience, smoother maintenance cycles, and enhanced network resiliency. When combined with robust routing policies, redundant network design, and coordinated use of complementary mechanisms like NSF and route dampening, Graceful Restart empowers operators to maintain high levels of service availability even in the face of routine maintenance or unexpected disruptions. Its adoption across service provider backbones, large-scale data centers, and enterprise networks underscores its effectiveness as a stabilizing force in the dynamic and interconnected world of BGP routing.

BGP Route Refresh Capability

The BGP Route Refresh capability is a fundamental enhancement to the Border Gateway Protocol that addresses a key operational challenge related to applying new routing policies on live BGP sessions. In traditional BGP implementations, once a session is established between two peers and routes have been exchanged, any policy changes that affect inbound routes typically require a full session reset to take effect. This means that network operators would need to manually tear down and re-establish the BGP session to trigger a new exchange of route advertisements reflecting the updated policies. The Route Refresh capability was introduced to eliminate this disruptive process by providing a non-intrusive mechanism for dynamically requesting updated routes from a peer without resetting the session.

Route Refresh was first introduced in RFC 2918 and later extended in RFC 7313 to support enhanced functionality. It allows a BGP router to request that its peer re-advertise previously sent routes so that the requesting router can reprocess those routes under new or modified policies. This capability is especially valuable in large-scale networks where session resets can result in significant route churn, convergence delays, and temporary service disruptions.

The mechanism is straightforward. During the initial BGP session negotiation, peers exchange OPEN messages that include capability advertisements. If both routers support Route Refresh, they indicate this in their capability negotiation. Once this capability is established, either peer can send a ROUTE-REFRESH message at any time during the session to request that the other peer resend its entire set of BGP advertisements. The refreshed routes are then processed by the receiving router under its current routing policies, including new prefix lists, route maps, or attribute manipulations that may have been configured since the initial session establishment.

In practical terms, Route Refresh is an essential tool for network engineers who need to implement real-time policy changes in production environments. For example, if an operator needs to adjust a route map that alters BGP attributes such as LOCAL_PREF, MED, or communities on inbound routes, they can deploy the change and issue a ROUTE-REFRESH request to the peer, ensuring that all relevant routes are re-evaluated under the new configuration. This avoids the need for a disruptive session reset, which in busy networks could impact traffic forwarding decisions and result in service instability.

Route Refresh also enhances operational flexibility. In dynamic network environments where traffic engineering requirements change frequently, being able to apply new routing policies on the fly is critical. Networks that participate in Internet Exchange Points, maintain multiple upstream peerings, or implement complex multi-tenant architectures benefit greatly from Route Refresh, as it allows them to adapt to evolving conditions without interrupting established sessions.

The extended version of Route Refresh, specified in RFC 7313, adds further functionality through the use of an End-of-RIB (End of Routing Information Base) marker. When a router sends a ROUTE-REFRESH message and the peer completes re-advertising all requested routes, it appends the End-of-RIB marker to signal that no further updates will follow. This marker ensures that the requesting router knows when the refresh process is complete, allowing for more efficient route processing and faster convergence times. Without the End-of-RIB marker, routers would need to rely on timers or assumptions about when the refresh cycle is finished.

Another advantage of Route Refresh is that it reduces the CPU and memory load on routers compared to traditional session resets. When a BGP session is reset, routers must tear down TCP connections, flush routing tables, and re-establish the session from scratch, processing all route advertisements again. This can introduce significant overhead, particularly when dealing with full Internet routing tables consisting of hundreds of thousands of prefixes. With Route Refresh, the session remains intact, and only the relevant routing information is reprocessed, saving both time and resources.

Despite its benefits, Route Refresh does require careful operational practices. When requesting a route refresh from a peer, especially one that is advertising a large number of prefixes, the reprocessing of routes can still result in temporary CPU spikes and increased load on the control plane. In large-scale networks, operators often schedule route refreshes during off-peak hours or stagger requests across multiple peers to minimize the impact on routing infrastructure.

It is also important to note that Route Refresh only applies to soft reconfiguration of inbound policies. Outbound policy changes—those affecting what routes a router advertises to its peers—still require the router to actively update its advertised routes. In many implementations, outbound policy changes automatically trigger new advertisements to peers without the need for Route Refresh, though this behavior can depend on the specific router's software version or vendor implementation.

An alternative to Route Refresh in older networks is the use of soft reconfiguration inbound. With soft reconfiguration, a router stores all received routes from a peer in memory, allowing administrators to apply new policies locally without requesting a re-advertisement. While this achieves a similar outcome, it comes at the cost of increased memory usage, as all received routes must be retained even if they are not installed in the forwarding table. In contrast, Route Refresh eliminates this additional memory overhead by allowing routers to dynamically request updates as needed.

Route Refresh has become a widely adopted standard in modern BGP networks and is supported by virtually all major router vendors. It is often combined with other BGP best practices, such as prefix filtering, community-based policies, and attribute manipulations, to enable fine-tuned control over route selection and traffic engineering.

In multi-tenant environments, cloud service providers, and large data centers, where route servers are commonly used to facilitate multilateral peering, Route Refresh ensures that policy updates can be implemented across dozens or even hundreds of peers efficiently. Route servers can receive refresh requests from participants, allowing for coordinated re-evaluation of routes according to the latest routing policies, without introducing instability into the peering fabric.

Overall, the BGP Route Refresh capability represents a critical improvement to the operational flexibility and stability of BGP deployments. By allowing dynamic re-evaluation of routing information without the need for disruptive session resets, Route Refresh enables network operators to apply routing policy updates with confidence, preserve session continuity, and maintain a more stable and responsive Internet routing infrastructure. As networks continue to scale and routing policies evolve more frequently, Route Refresh will remain an essential feature for maintaining agile and resilient BGP operations.

BGP and IPv6

As the world transitions from IPv4 to IPv6, the Border Gateway Protocol continues to be the cornerstone of inter-domain routing. The exponential growth of devices, users, and services on the Internet has driven the demand for a larger address space than what IPv4 can provide. IPv6, with its 128-bit address structure, addresses this challenge by offering an almost inexhaustible pool of IP addresses.

However, the introduction of IPv6 required enhancements and adaptations within BGP to support the new protocol effectively. While the fundamental mechanisms of BGP remain unchanged, its interaction with IPv6 introduces unique considerations and operational nuances.

BGP supports IPv6 through the Multiprotocol Extensions for BGP, defined in RFC 4760. These extensions allow BGP to advertise routing information for multiple network layer protocols, including IPv6, alongside traditional IPv4 prefixes. This is achieved by using Address Family Identifier (AFI) and Subsequent Address Family Identifier (SAFI) values to distinguish between IPv4 and IPv6 route advertisements. For IPv6, AFI 2 with SAFI 1 is used to signal unicast IPv6 reachability information. With these extensions in place, BGP routers can simultaneously handle IPv4 and IPv6 routing tables, making it possible to deploy dual-stack environments where both protocols operate in parallel.

One of the primary operational changes when implementing BGP for IPv6 is the establishment of BGP sessions over IPv6 transport. Unlike legacy BGP sessions that typically use IPv4 as the underlying transport layer, IPv6-enabled BGP peers can establish sessions using IPv6 link-local or global unicast addresses. However, it is also common practice for BGP routers to maintain IPv4 transport sessions while exchanging both IPv4 and IPv6 routing information over the same session using multiprotocol extensions. This flexibility allows network operators to incrementally transition their networks to IPv6 while retaining backward compatibility with IPv4.

IPv6 introduces new considerations related to next-hop reachability. In IPv4 BGP, the next-hop attribute usually points to an IPv4 address that must be reachable within the Interior Gateway Protocol (IGP). In IPv6 BGP, the next-hop address is typically an IPv6 global or link-local address, and its reachability must also be assured by the local IGP, such as OSPFv3 or IS-IS for IPv6. Furthermore, when using link-local addresses as next hops, both routers must be directly connected, and the specific outgoing interface must be specified in the configuration. These details require careful planning to ensure seamless routing and forwarding of IPv6 traffic.

Route aggregation remains a critical tool in managing the growth of the IPv6 global routing table. Similar to IPv4, IPv6 BGP supports route summarization to reduce the number of advertised prefixes and improve the efficiency of routing tables. However, due to the abundance of available address space in IPv6, many organizations are allocated large address blocks, such as /32 or /48 prefixes, from Regional Internet Registries. Without responsible aggregation practices, the potential for rapid growth in the IPv6 routing table is significant. Network operators are encouraged to summarize prefixes where possible and avoid excessive de-aggregation to ensure the scalability of the Internet's routing infrastructure.

The adoption of IPv6 has also necessitated changes in BGP security and policy controls. Filtering IPv6 prefixes at BGP session boundaries is essential to prevent route leaks, hijacks, and the advertisement of unauthorized prefixes. Prefix lists, route maps, and RPKI origin validation should be applied to both IPv4 and IPv6 BGP sessions. The introduction of IPv6 has prompted organizations to review and update their routing policies, ensuring that IPv6 prefixes receive the same level of scrutiny and control as their IPv4 counterparts.

Another significant development is the deployment of IPv6-only networks. As IPv6 adoption increases, some organizations are exploring the use of IPv6 as the sole transport and addressing protocol, particularly within internal networks or new data center builds. In these environments, BGP plays a crucial role in distributing IPv6 routing information across the backbone and facilitating interconnection with external IPv6-enabled networks. IPv6-only designs simplify network operations by removing the need to maintain dual-stack configurations, reducing complexity and operational overhead.

BGP's role in IPv6-enabled Content Delivery Networks and cloud infrastructures is especially prominent. As user demand for IPv6 connectivity grows, CDNs and cloud providers must ensure that their platforms support native IPv6 transport. This involves configuring BGP to advertise IPv6 routes from edge locations to upstream transit providers and Internet Exchange Points. The ability to deliver content natively over IPv6 improves performance by avoiding translation mechanisms such as NAT64 or protocol tunnels, reducing latency and enhancing the end-user experience.

Operational monitoring and troubleshooting of IPv6 BGP sessions follow similar principles to IPv4 but with additional IPv6-specific considerations. Network engineers must verify IPv6 neighbor reachability, monitor next-hop availability, and analyze advertised IPv6 prefixes. Looking glass servers and route collectors increasingly offer visibility into global IPv6 route propagation, allowing operators to confirm the reachability and visibility of their IPv6 prefixes across the Internet.

Despite steady progress, the global deployment of IPv6 via BGP has not been without challenges. The coexistence of IPv4 and IPv6 in dual-stack networks introduces complexity, as routing policies, traffic engineering strategies, and security controls must be duplicated across both protocols. Additionally, while IPv6 adoption continues to grow, some regions and service providers still maintain limited IPv6 support, requiring networks to implement transition technologies such as 6PE (IPv6 Provider Edge), 6RD (Rapid Deployment), or GRE tunnels to bridge gaps between IPv6 islands.

Traffic engineering with IPv6 BGP attributes, such as LOCAL_PREF, MED, AS_PATH prepending, and BGP communities, mirrors their IPv4 counterparts. However, operators must be vigilant to ensure that IPv6-specific traffic engineering policies align with organizational goals, particularly when managing multi-homed environments with both IPv4 and IPv6 peering. Balancing IPv4 and IPv6 traffic flows and ensuring parity in routing behavior across both protocols is key to maintaining consistent network performance.

Ultimately, BGP has proven to be a versatile and adaptable protocol, enabling the Internet's smooth transition from IPv4 to IPv6. Its ability to scale, incorporate multiprotocol capabilities, and support granular routing policies has made it the preferred protocol for global IPv6 route distribution. As the Internet moves further toward a future where IPv6 is the dominant addressing scheme, BGP will remain the backbone of inter-domain routing, ensuring the connectivity, stability, and scalability of the next-generation Internet. The continued expansion of IPv6 BGP peering relationships and the optimization of IPv6 routing policies will play a vital role in shaping the evolution of modern network infrastructures.

Segment Routing and BGP

Segment Routing has emerged as a significant advancement in network traffic engineering and service delivery, providing a scalable and flexible mechanism for steering traffic through a network. Traditionally, MPLS and RSVP-TE have been the go-to technologies for traffic engineering in large-scale service provider and enterprise networks. However, these technologies come with operational complexity, signaling overhead, and scalability challenges. Segment Routing simplifies the traffic engineering process by encoding the path that a packet should follow directly into the packet itself using segment identifiers. When integrated with BGP, Segment Routing enables a more dynamic and programmable network architecture, allowing operators to optimize traffic flows and service delivery without relying on complex control plane signaling.

At its core, Segment Routing introduces the concept of segments, which are instructions associated with specific network nodes or functions. These segments can represent topological information, such as a particular node or interface, or service instructions, such as applying specific network policies or steering traffic through defined waypoints. In MPLS-based Segment Routing, known as SR-MPLS, these segments are encoded as MPLS labels, while in IPv6-based Segment Routing, known as SRv6, segments are encoded in the IPv6 Segment Routing Header (SRH).

The relationship between BGP and Segment Routing lies in the distribution of routing information and the advertisement of segment identifiers throughout the network. BGP is extended to support Segment Routing through mechanisms such as BGP-LS (BGP Link-State) and BGP SR-TE (Segment Routing Traffic Engineering). BGP-LS enables BGP to carry link-state information learned from IGPs like OSPF or IS-IS and distribute it to external controllers or route reflectors. This link-state database can then be used by centralized controllers to compute optimized paths and generate Segment Routing policies.

BGP SR-TE takes this a step further by enabling routers to advertise Segment Routing Traffic Engineering policies directly to their BGP peers. These policies define explicit paths composed of a sequence of segments that a packet must traverse. Operators can use BGP SR-TE to dynamically inject end-to-end traffic engineering instructions into the network without requiring traditional RSVP-TE signaling. This shift toward a BGP-driven control plane for traffic engineering brings the benefits of simplification and scalability to the network, as BGP's mature policy control mechanisms are already widely deployed and understood by operators.

One of the key advantages of integrating Segment Routing with BGP is the improved programmability it offers for service providers and large enterprises. By leveraging a BGP-based control plane to distribute Segment Routing policies, operators can dynamically adjust traffic flows in response to real-time network conditions, such as congestion, failures, or latency variations. For example, a centralized SDN controller can use BGP SR-TE to push new segment lists to ingress routers, steering high-priority traffic along less congested or lower-latency paths without requiring manual reconfiguration of routers or intervention in the underlying IGP.

Additionally, Segment Routing enhances the deployment of network slicing and service chaining, two key components of modern network architectures such as 5G. In network slicing, operators create virtualized and isolated logical networks, or slices, over shared physical infrastructure. Segment Routing enables each slice to have its own traffic engineering and service policies, encoded as segment lists that guide packets through the appropriate virtualized network functions and physical nodes. With BGP serving as the distribution protocol for these segment lists, operators can easily propagate slice-specific instructions across the network, simplifying the management of complex multi-tenant or multi-service environments.

Service chaining is another area where Segment Routing and BGP play a vital role. In traditional service chaining, packets are steered through a series of middleboxes, such as firewalls, load balancers, or deep packet inspection devices, using manual configurations or tunneling mechanisms. With Segment Routing, these service chains can be encoded directly into packets using segment lists that identify each service node along the path. BGP policies can distribute these service chains dynamically to network devices, enabling highly automated and flexible service delivery.

From an operational perspective, the integration of BGP and Segment Routing allows for granular policy control. Operators can apply BGP routing policies to influence how and when Segment Routing policies are distributed to peers or internal routers. For instance, specific SR-TE policies may only be advertised to routers within a particular region, data center, or tenant, allowing for localized optimization and customized service levels.

Segment Routing also provides failover and resiliency advantages. By defining primary and backup segment lists, BGP can be used to advertise multiple candidate paths to an ingress router. In the event of a network failure or degraded link performance, the ingress router can switch to an alternative segment list without waiting for global IGP convergence. This local protection mechanism reduces recovery times and minimizes traffic disruption.

In modern networks, especially those leveraging automation and orchestration platforms, Segment Routing and BGP are integral to intent-based networking. Through northbound APIs, SDN controllers can interface with BGP-enabled routers to automatically compute and deploy Segment Routing policies in line with business objectives and service level agreements. This tight integration reduces the operational burden on network engineers and accelerates the deployment of new services.

BGP's role in carrying Segment Routing policies also enhances visibility and monitoring capabilities. By advertising segment lists and SR-TE policies as part of BGP updates, network operators can leverage existing BGP monitoring tools to track the distribution and activation of Segment Routing paths. Telemetry data collected from routers provides insights into path utilization, segment list effectiveness, and potential areas of network congestion, enabling data-driven optimizations.

With the increasing adoption of SR-MPLS and SRv6, BGP's role as a universal control plane for inter-domain and intra-domain routing continues to expand. The protocol's ability to manage IPv4, IPv6, and MPLS reachability, combined with its new responsibilities in Segment Routing policy distribution, reinforces its position as the central component of modern, software-defined networks.

Ultimately, the integration of Segment Routing and BGP transforms the way networks handle traffic engineering and service delivery. The reduction in complexity, enhanced scalability, and improved agility empower service providers and large enterprises to meet the demands of cloud-native applications, real-time services, and digital transformation initiatives. By combining BGP's well-established routing capabilities with the innovative flexibility of Segment Routing, operators can build networks that are not only more efficient and resilient but also more responsive to changing business and technological requirements.

The Role of BGP in SDN

The rise of Software-Defined Networking has significantly changed the way networks are designed, managed, and operated. SDN introduces the concept of separating the control plane from the data plane, enabling centralized network control, dynamic programmability, and automation. Despite the emergence of new protocols and frameworks within SDN environments, the Border Gateway Protocol remains an essential component of many SDN architectures, playing a critical role in routing, policy distribution, and overall network orchestration. BGP's flexibility, scalability, and mature ecosystem make it well-suited for integration into SDN models, where it continues to serve as a cornerstone for inter-domain and intra-domain routing.

One of the main ways BGP integrates into SDN is by acting as the southbound interface between the SDN controller and the network devices. While traditional SDN implementations often rely on protocols like OpenFlow to control forwarding behavior, BGP provides a familiar and standardized way for controllers to program routing tables and steer traffic. In many modern SDN deployments, particularly in carrier and data center networks, controllers use BGP to communicate routing information to routers and switches, leveraging the protocol's path vector mechanism to distribute reachability data and influence path selection across the network fabric.

A practical example of this integration can be found in SDN-based IP/MPLS networks. In these environments, centralized SDN controllers compute optimal paths for traffic flows based on network policies, topology information, and real-time telemetry. The controller then uses BGP to distribute these paths to Provider Edge (PE) routers or other edge devices, effectively functioning as a Route Reflector or centralized BGP speaker. This approach allows operators to automate traffic engineering, service provisioning, and failover mechanisms without relying on traditional distributed control planes.

BGP-LS, or BGP Link-State, is one of the key extensions that bridges BGP and SDN. BGP-LS enables routers running link-state protocols like OSPF or IS-IS to export link-state and topology information to an SDN controller using BGP updates. This provides the controller with a comprehensive view of the network's topology, enabling it to compute and enforce intelligent routing decisions. Once the controller determines the optimal paths, it can use BGP-based policies, such as BGP SR-TE (Segment Routing Traffic Engineering), to install those paths into the network devices. The combination of BGP-LS and BGP SR-TE gives SDN controllers the power to optimize traffic flows dynamically while reducing operational overhead.

Another important role BGP plays in SDN is within multi-domain or hybrid environments. Many organizations adopting SDN operate networks that span traditional infrastructure and newer SDN-controlled segments. BGP serves as a common language between these domains, ensuring seamless interoperability. For instance, a traditional service provider backbone running conventional BGP can connect to an SDN-controlled data center via standard BGP peering. This allows SDN-managed networks to advertise their prefixes to external peers, while also learning external routes from upstream providers or partners using the same well-established BGP mechanisms.

In data center environments, SDN and BGP coexist in designs such as EVPN (Ethernet VPN) over VXLAN. In EVPN-VXLAN fabrics, BGP is used to distribute both Layer 2 and Layer 3 reachability information between leaf and spine switches. The SDN controller typically manages the overlay network, automating the deployment of VXLAN tunnels and EVPN route advertisements. BGP plays a crucial role here by disseminating MAC address and IP prefix information, ensuring that tenant workloads can communicate efficiently across the data center fabric. This approach allows data centers to scale horizontally while maintaining seamless workload mobility, tenant isolation, and efficient east-west traffic flow.

The programmability benefits of SDN are further enhanced when BGP is integrated into network automation workflows. SDN controllers or network orchestration platforms can leverage BGP's policy control capabilities to automatically adjust routing behavior based on predefined intents or real-time analytics. For example, if an SDN controller detects congestion on a specific link, it can dynamically adjust BGP route preferences by modifying LOCAL_PREF attributes or applying AS_PATH prepending to steer traffic along alternate paths. This level of automation enables operators to maintain service level agreements and optimize network performance without manual intervention.

Security also benefits from the fusion of BGP and SDN. With centralized control, SDN controllers can enforce strict routing and security policies across the network through BGP updates. These policies can include prefix filtering, route validation, and RPKI enforcement, ensuring that only authorized and validated routes are accepted by network devices. Additionally, SDN-controlled networks can implement service chaining using BGP communities or Segment Routing-based instructions, directing traffic through firewalls, load balancers, or other security appliances before reaching its destination.

The emergence of cloud-native applications and distributed microservices architectures has also increased the demand for programmable networks where BGP and SDN coexist. Public cloud providers, for instance, often use BGP as a core protocol for customer connectivity via direct peering services like AWS Direct Connect, Azure ExpressRoute, or Google Cloud Interconnect. These cloud providers implement SDN within their internal infrastructure while leveraging BGP to manage external routing relationships with customers. The combination allows for dynamic route exchange and seamless integration of customer networks into the cloud provider's SDN-controlled environment.

Furthermore, BGP enables multi-tenant isolation and scalability within SDN environments. By using BGP communities, route targets, and VPNv4/VPNv6 address families, SDN controllers can manage multiple virtual networks or slices over a shared physical infrastructure. Each tenant or service can be assigned its own set of BGP policies, route distinguishers, and import/export rules to ensure isolation and compliance with specific service-level requirements.

Operationally, BGP simplifies SDN troubleshooting and observability. Many traditional network monitoring tools, such as BGP route collectors, looking glasses, and telemetry platforms, can continue to operate in SDN-enabled environments. By analyzing BGP updates, route advertisements, and path selections, operators gain visibility into the behavior of both the SDN control plane and the data plane, enabling proactive issue detection and resolution.

Despite the newer protocols introduced by SDN architectures, BGP's continued relevance is rooted in its flexibility, extensibility, and widespread adoption across diverse networking environments. From WAN backbones to cloud networks and data centers, BGP remains the protocol of choice for scalable and policy-driven route distribution. In SDN ecosystems, it complements the controller's centralized intelligence by providing a proven and interoperable mechanism for programming routing information across devices.

As networks evolve toward intent-based, programmable architectures, BGP will remain a critical enabler, facilitating the seamless integration of traditional and SDN-controlled domains. Its role in automating network behavior, distributing service policies, and optimizing traffic flows will continue to expand, reinforcing its position as a vital component of modern SDN designs. The synergy between BGP and SDN creates a foundation for building networks that are not only more efficient and agile but also better aligned with the dynamic requirements of today's digital landscape.

BGP in Content Delivery Networks

Content Delivery Networks play a critical role in delivering digital content efficiently and reliably to users around the world. Whether it is streaming video, serving website assets, or distributing software updates, CDNs are designed to bring content closer to end-users by leveraging a globally distributed network of edge servers. The Border Gateway Protocol is one of the foundational technologies that allows CDNs to function effectively, facilitating the routing and optimization of traffic between CDN edge locations and the broader Internet. BGP enables CDN operators to manage traffic flows, implement traffic engineering policies, and optimize user experience by ensuring content is delivered via the most optimal paths.

At the heart of a CDN's architecture is its network of strategically placed edge nodes or Points of Presence. These nodes cache and deliver content to end-users, minimizing latency and reducing the load on origin servers. To ensure that user requests are routed to the nearest or most efficient edge node, CDNs rely heavily on BGP's ability to influence routing decisions on the Internet. By advertising IP prefixes from multiple edge locations to various upstream providers, Internet exchanges, and peer networks, CDNs control how traffic is steered toward their infrastructure.

One of the key techniques used by CDNs is Anycast routing, which leverages BGP to advertise the same IP prefix from multiple geographically dispersed edge nodes. When a user sends a request to an Anycast IP address, BGP ensures that the traffic is routed to the nearest or most optimal node based on the Internet's routing topology. This model allows CDNs to reduce latency by serving content from the closest available edge node, improving page load times, video streaming quality, and overall user satisfaction. Anycast also provides inherent redundancy and load balancing, as traffic will automatically shift to alternative nodes in the event of network failures or congestion.

BGP communities are another essential tool used by CDNs to implement advanced traffic engineering policies. By tagging routes with specific BGP community values, CDN operators can signal preferences to upstream providers, peers, and Internet exchange points. These community tags can be used to control route propagation, prefer or de-prefer certain routes, or influence local preference settings on upstream routers. For example, a CDN might use BGP communities to ensure that traffic destined for a particular region is only advertised to local ISPs within that region, preventing suboptimal routing through distant transit providers.

In addition to influencing inbound traffic toward CDN edge nodes, BGP also plays a critical role in outbound traffic engineering. When CDN nodes need to fetch content from origin servers or communicate with other parts of the CDN infrastructure, BGP attributes such as LOCAL_PREF, MED, and AS_PATH prepending are used to shape outbound traffic flows. This helps CDNs optimize their internal network performance and manage bandwidth costs, especially when dealing with multiple upstream transit providers and peering partners.

Peering at Internet Exchange Points is a fundamental strategy for CDN operators to enhance performance and reduce costs. By directly connecting to multiple ISPs and content consumers via IXPs, CDNs can deliver traffic more efficiently, bypassing transit providers and shortening the path to end-users. BGP is the protocol that establishes and maintains these peering sessions, enabling the exchange of routing information and facilitating direct traffic flows. This approach not only reduces latency but also allows CDN operators to better manage traffic surges, particularly during events such as software launches, sports broadcasts, or viral content spikes.

BGP route optimization is another critical component of CDN operations. CDNs often deploy route optimization platforms that analyze network telemetry, including latency measurements, packet loss statistics, and real-time congestion data. Based on this analysis, CDN operators can dynamically adjust BGP attributes to steer traffic away from congested or degraded paths toward more optimal routes. These changes are often automated, enabling real-time adjustments to accommodate fluctuating Internet conditions and ensure consistent service quality for users.

Global resiliency and disaster recovery are further enhanced through BGP's capabilities. By maintaining multiple edge locations that advertise the same or overlapping IP prefixes via BGP, CDNs ensure that failures in one location do not result in service disruptions. If an edge node becomes unavailable due to hardware failure, power outage, or network issues, BGP automatically redirects traffic to the next closest or best-performing node without requiring intervention from users or applications.

In highly distributed CDNs with hundreds of edge nodes, managing BGP policies and sessions can become complex. Automation and orchestration platforms are critical in maintaining consistent and scalable BGP configurations across all locations. These platforms enable centralized management of BGP policies, session parameters, and community tagging, ensuring that the entire CDN network behaves as intended, even as new edge nodes are deployed or traffic patterns evolve.

Security is also a major consideration in BGP's role within CDNs. CDNs are frequent targets of Distributed Denial-of-Service (DDoS) attacks due to the scale of traffic they handle and the critical content they deliver. BGP provides mechanisms to mitigate the impact of such attacks, including blackhole routing and remote triggered blackholing. In the event of a volumetric attack targeting a specific prefix, CDN operators can signal upstream providers to discard attack traffic upstream using BGP-triggered blackholing, preserving network availability and protecting other parts of the infrastructure.

RPKI-based route origin validation is becoming a standard practice for CDN operators to secure their BGP advertisements. By signing IP prefixes with cryptographic Route Origin Authorizations (ROAs), CDNs ensure that only authorized ASes can originate their prefixes, reducing the risk of route hijacking incidents that could redirect user traffic to malicious actors or cause widespread outages.

Beyond public CDNs, enterprise networks that deploy private or hybrid CDN architectures also rely on BGP to manage routing between private data centers, cloud providers, and edge caches. These enterprises often extend their BGP policies into cloud environments using direct connections such as AWS Direct Connect or Azure ExpressRoute. In this context, BGP provides seamless route exchange between the enterprise's private network and the CDN's edge infrastructure, ensuring efficient content distribution and optimal traffic flows for internal applications and external-facing services.

BGP's enduring role within CDN architectures highlights its adaptability and importance in large-scale, distributed networks. Its ability to influence routing decisions, support Anycast deployments, facilitate direct peering, and enable real-time traffic optimization makes it indispensable to CDN operations. As Internet usage continues to grow and the demand for high-performance, low-latency content delivery intensifies, BGP will remain a critical enabler in helping CDNs deliver reliable, scalable, and efficient services to users worldwide.

BGP for DDoS Mitigation

The Border Gateway Protocol plays a crucial role in mitigating Distributed Denial-of-Service attacks, which continue to be one of the most pervasive and damaging threats to network infrastructure and online services. As DDoS attacks grow in scale and sophistication, organizations have turned to BGP-based techniques to help protect their networks from becoming overwhelmed. By leveraging BGP's ability to dynamically influence routing decisions, operators can redirect or filter malicious traffic at the network edge or upstream provider level, limiting the impact on their internal infrastructure and preserving service availability for legitimate users.

One of the most common BGP-based strategies for DDoS mitigation is remote triggered blackholing. This method involves injecting specially marked BGP routes into the network, instructing routers to discard traffic destined for the target IP prefixes before it reaches the victim's infrastructure. Blackhole routes typically carry a next-hop IP address set to a null interface, such as Nullo, effectively dropping all traffic to that destination. In remote triggered blackholing, the victim network or its upstream provider advertises these routes upstream, allowing traffic to be dropped closer to its source and reducing congestion on transit links.

To automate and streamline this process, many networks use BGP communities to tag prefixes that require blackholing. These communities are recognized by upstream providers or Internet exchange route servers, which then apply the appropriate routing policies to discard the traffic at their edge routers. This enables rapid response to DDoS incidents, often in a matter of minutes, without requiring manual intervention on every affected router. By stopping attack traffic before it consumes critical bandwidth or overwhelms internal systems, remote triggered blackholing helps organizations maintain operational stability during an attack.

While effective, blackholing has the downside of making the targeted prefix completely unreachable, affecting both legitimate and malicious traffic alike. To address this limitation, more advanced techniques such as BGP diversion or traffic scrubbing are often used. In BGP diversion, also known as BGP FlowSpec diversion, the victim's traffic is redirected to a dedicated scrubbing center where malicious traffic is filtered, and clean traffic is returned to the customer network. This redirection is done by injecting BGP updates that steer traffic for the target prefix to the mitigation provider's infrastructure, where deep packet inspection and traffic filtering tools analyze incoming flows.

FlowSpec, defined in RFC 5575, is a powerful extension to BGP that allows operators to distribute granular traffic filtering policies across their networks. FlowSpec enables routers to match on specific fields within packet headers, such as source or destination IP addresses, port numbers, protocols, and more. By using BGP to advertise FlowSpec rules, operators can dynamically deploy traffic filtering in response to DDoS attacks, blocking or rate-limiting specific attack vectors, such as UDP floods, TCP SYN floods, or DNS amplification attempts, without affecting legitimate traffic flows.

One of the key benefits of using BGP FlowSpec is its speed and scalability. Operators can propagate filtering rules to multiple routers across the network within seconds, ensuring a coordinated and widespread defense against volumetric attacks. This is particularly valuable in large service provider networks or in cloud environments where DDoS attacks can target multiple locations simultaneously. FlowSpec also complements traditional access control lists and firewall rules by offering greater automation and reduced operational overhead during attack mitigation.

In addition to remote triggered blackholing and FlowSpec, BGP communities play an important role in coordinating DDoS mitigation efforts between organizations and their upstream providers. Many transit providers define well-known BGP communities that customers can use to signal mitigation requests. These communities can instruct the provider to implement actions such as selective blackholing, rate-limiting, or diverting traffic to scrubbing centers. This flexibility allows customers to tailor their mitigation strategies according to the nature of the attack and the business impact on the targeted service.

Another key use case for BGP in DDoS mitigation is within the context of Anycast networks. Many global service providers and content delivery networks use Anycast routing to advertise the same IP prefix from multiple geographically dispersed locations. During a DDoS attack, Anycast's inherent traffic distribution capabilities help spread the attack load across multiple sites, reducing the impact on any single location. By coupling Anycast with BGP routing policies, operators can dynamically withdraw or de-prefer routes for affected nodes, steering traffic away from compromised or overloaded infrastructure to healthier locations.

Beyond protecting against volumetric attacks, BGP-based mitigation strategies are also effective in defending against more sophisticated application-layer attacks. By combining BGP route manipulation with traffic analysis, operators can identify and isolate suspicious traffic patterns originating from specific regions or networks. BGP can then be used to de-prefer or block routes from these regions, reducing the surface area for further attacks.

Additionally, many DDoS mitigation providers integrate BGP signaling into their mitigation platforms. These providers often operate large scrubbing centers capable of absorbing and filtering terabits of malicious traffic. When a customer detects an attack, they can automatically or manually initiate a BGP route announcement that diverts attack traffic to the provider's infrastructure. After scrubbing, clean traffic is delivered to the customer via tunnels or private links. This model, known as BGP-based upstream mitigation, provides a robust defense against large-scale attacks while preserving service availability for legitimate users.

For organizations that operate hybrid networks combining on-premises data centers and public cloud resources, BGP also facilitates cross-environment DDoS mitigation strategies. Enterprises can use

BGP to selectively route traffic between on-premises and cloud-based scrubbing services, ensuring flexible protection based on where services are hosted. For example, an enterprise may implement BGP diversion to send traffic to a cloud-based scrubbing service during peak attack periods, while relying on local blackholing for less severe incidents.

While BGP-based DDoS mitigation techniques are powerful, they are not without challenges. Misconfigurations, such as incorrect blackhole advertisements or overly broad FlowSpec rules, can lead to unintended service disruptions. Therefore, careful planning, automated validation, and comprehensive monitoring are essential components of a successful BGP-driven mitigation strategy. Operators must also ensure that routing security practices, such as RPKI-based route origin validation, are in place to prevent attackers from hijacking mitigation prefixes or manipulating BGP routes during an attack.

Ultimately, BGP's adaptability and wide deployment across the Internet make it an indispensable tool in the fight against DDoS attacks. Its ability to distribute mitigation policies rapidly, influence traffic flows, and coordinate with upstream providers and mitigation services gives organizations the control they need to defend against increasingly complex threats. As the threat landscape evolves and attackers develop new tactics, BGP will continue to serve as a vital component of multi-layered DDoS defense strategies, helping safeguard critical infrastructure and online services.

BGP and Anycast Deployments

The Border Gateway Protocol plays a central role in enabling Anycast deployments, a routing methodology that allows multiple, geographically distributed nodes to advertise the same IP prefix. This approach is widely used in modern Internet architectures to improve network resilience, optimize user experience, and reduce latency by ensuring that users are connected to the nearest available instance of a service. Anycast routing leverages BGP's global reach and path selection capabilities to direct user traffic to the closest node based on the network topology, routing policies, and dynamic conditions on the Internet.

At its core, Anycast involves advertising the same IP prefix from multiple locations, with each location running a service instance that is identical in terms of functionality and content. These instances could be edge servers in a content delivery network, DNS resolvers, or application frontends. The BGP routers at each location announce the shared prefix to their upstream providers or peering partners. Because BGP selects routes based on path attributes such as AS_PATH length, LOCAL_PREF, and policy preferences, traffic from end-users is routed to the nearest or most optimal node based on these BGP decisions.

One of the primary benefits of Anycast, when implemented with BGP, is the inherent traffic distribution it provides. Rather than centralizing traffic to a single data center or node, Anycast disperses requests across multiple nodes, reducing the load on individual servers and improving redundancy. In the event that one node becomes unavailable due to network failure, maintenance, or overload, BGP's convergence mechanisms will automatically withdraw the affected route, redirecting traffic to the next closest available node without requiring changes at the client side. This creates a self-healing, distributed infrastructure that significantly improves service uptime and resilience.

BGP's flexibility in route manipulation makes Anycast even more powerful. By using techniques such as AS_PATH prepending or BGP community tagging, network operators can influence the way traffic flows into the Anycast nodes. For example, an operator might prepend additional AS numbers to the BGP advertisements of a specific node to make it less preferred for certain regions or networks, effectively steering traffic to alternative locations. This level of control enables precise tuning of Anycast behavior, allowing operators to balance load across nodes or adapt to regional differences in network performance.

In global deployments, Anycast helps solve the challenge of delivering consistent and low-latency services to users in different geographical regions. DNS providers, for instance, commonly use Anycast to ensure that queries are resolved by the closest DNS server, minimizing query resolution times and improving end-user performance. Similarly, content delivery networks rely on Anycast to ensure that users retrieve content from the nearest edge cache, reducing round-trip times and accelerating content delivery.

BGP's role in Anycast deployments is also critical to improving DDoS mitigation and network security. Because Anycast distributes traffic across multiple nodes, it helps absorb and diffuse the impact of volumetric attacks. When attackers attempt to flood an Anycasted service with traffic, the attack is inherently fragmented across all the nodes advertising the Anycast prefix. This limits the damage to any single node and helps maintain service availability in other regions. Additionally, operators can temporarily withdraw BGP advertisements from affected nodes during an attack, redirecting traffic to alternative nodes that may be protected by additional mitigation infrastructure, such as scrubbing centers.

The deployment of Anycast using BGP requires careful consideration of node placement and routing policies. Nodes should be strategically located in regions with high user density or close to major peering exchanges and transit providers to maximize the benefits of localized routing. BGP session policies, maximum prefix limits, and ingress/egress filtering rules must be configured to ensure stable and secure route propagation. Operators also need to monitor the health and reachability of each node, as well as the performance of BGP sessions, to detect anomalies or routing issues that could affect Anycast performance.

In multi-provider environments, where Anycast nodes peer with multiple upstream ISPs or Internet exchanges, BGP allows operators to take advantage of diverse peering ecosystems. By advertising Anycast prefixes through different providers, operators can optimize how traffic enters the network from various regions or autonomous systems. This multi-homed approach increases resilience against single-provider outages and enhances global route diversity, helping to ensure that user traffic always has an efficient path to the service.

Operationally, managing Anycast deployments requires robust telemetry and monitoring solutions. Since BGP does not inherently provide visibility into which node users are being routed to, operators rely on a combination of network monitoring tools, application-layer logging, and traceroute analysis to gain insights into traffic distribution patterns. These insights are essential for troubleshooting routing anomalies, optimizing node selection, and ensuring that users are consistently routed to the most appropriate Anycast node.

Another dimension of BGP and Anycast deployments is their role in hybrid cloud and edge computing environments. Many organizations deploy Anycasted services across both on-premises infrastructure and public cloud platforms, with BGP facilitating seamless routing between them. This allows enterprises to leverage the global reach and scalability of cloud providers while maintaining control over critical services hosted in private data centers. In edge computing scenarios, Anycast combined with BGP ensures that user requests are processed at the closest edge location, reducing the need for data to traverse long network paths to centralized data centers.

BGP-based Anycast is also integral to critical Internet infrastructure, such as Root DNS servers and other essential public services. These services rely on globally distributed Anycast nodes to ensure that they remain available even under severe network stress or malicious attacks. The stability and resilience provided by BGP-driven Anycast routing are key to maintaining the health and reliability of the broader Internet ecosystem.

Finally, as networks continue to evolve, operators are exploring ways to enhance Anycast deployments through automation and intent-based networking. SDN controllers and orchestration platforms are increasingly integrated with BGP to automate the deployment of Anycast prefixes, dynamically adjust routing policies, and respond in real time to network conditions. This level of automation allows networks to scale more efficiently, adapt to traffic fluctuations, and reduce manual operational overhead.

BGP's ability to support Anycast at scale has made it an indispensable tool for organizations that demand high-performance, resilient, and globally distributed services. By enabling intelligent routing decisions, fast failover capabilities, and fine-grained control over traffic engineering, BGP continues to be the protocol of choice for powering modern Anycast deployments across a wide array of applications, from

DNS and content delivery to security services and cloud-native infrastructures.

BGP and Network Automation

The integration of the Border Gateway Protocol with network automation has transformed the way modern networks are designed, operated, and maintained. As networks continue to scale in size and complexity, manual configuration and troubleshooting of BGP have become inefficient and error-prone. Automation, therefore, plays a critical role in enabling organizations to deploy BGP faster, maintain consistency across devices, implement complex routing policies, and improve operational efficiency. BGP, being one of the most widely used protocols in service provider and enterprise networks, benefits greatly from automation frameworks, scripting, and orchestration platforms that streamline configuration, monitoring, and management tasks.

Traditionally, BGP configurations were applied manually via command-line interfaces, requiring engineers to input neighbor relationships, policy controls, prefix-lists, and route maps for every peer or autonomous system. As the number of BGP peers grows, especially in large-scale networks with hundreds of peering sessions or dynamic multi-tenant environments, this manual approach increases the risk of misconfigurations. Errors such as mismatched AS numbers, incorrect route filters, or missing authentication keys can cause session failures, routing anomalies, or even network-wide outages. By adopting automation, network operators can mitigate these risks by defining standardized templates and workflows that ensure consistency across BGP configurations.

Infrastructure as Code (IaC) is one of the most effective automation methodologies used to manage BGP deployments. With IaC tools like Ansible, Terraform, or SaltStack, network teams can codify BGP configurations into reusable templates, making it easy to deploy or modify BGP sessions programmatically across a fleet of routers. These tools enable operators to define variables for BGP peers, AS numbers, password settings, maximum prefix limits, and routing policies, then automatically generate and apply the configurations on multiple devices. This reduces manual workload and eliminates configuration drift, where discrepancies emerge between intended and actual configurations on network devices.

Beyond initial configuration, automation is essential in managing the full lifecycle of BGP operations. For example, automating BGP peer validation processes ensures that each session is properly authenticated, configured, and monitored. Automated scripts or orchestration platforms can validate that all peers are using correct MD5 keys or TCP-AO, verify that prefix-lists are up to date, and check that route policies are aligned with organizational standards. Automation also allows operators to quickly onboard new peers or customers by generating and applying complete BGP configurations in minutes, rather than hours or days.

In modern data centers and cloud environments, BGP automation extends into dynamic network provisioning. Cloud providers and large enterprises use automation frameworks to integrate BGP into their SDN platforms, enabling dynamic route advertisement and withdrawal as workloads spin up or down. For instance, in a Kubernetes-based environment using MetalLB or Calico, BGP speakers automatically advertise service IPs or pod networks to external routers, ensuring seamless north-south traffic flows. Automation tools orchestrate this process, eliminating the need for manual BGP reconfiguration when applications scale or migrate between nodes.

Network automation also plays a vital role in BGP-based traffic engineering. Operators can leverage APIs and automation workflows to adjust routing policies based on real-time network conditions, such as link utilization, latency metrics, or service-level objectives. For example, if a link becomes congested, automated workflows can dynamically modify LOCAL_PREF attributes or apply AS_PATH prepending to reroute traffic along less congested paths. Automation platforms integrated with telemetry systems enable these adjustments to occur within seconds, optimizing traffic flows while reducing manual intervention.

Monitoring and observability are critical components of BGP automation. Network operators increasingly rely on automated telemetry collection to gather real-time data on BGP session health, route changes, prefix counts, and anomalies. Streaming telemetry protocols such as gRPC or NETCONF/YANG models enable network devices to send BGP metrics directly to telemetry collectors, where automation scripts or platforms like Prometheus or Grafana process and visualize the data. With automated alerting based on predefined thresholds or anomaly detection algorithms, network teams can respond rapidly to session flaps, routing leaks, or hijacks, minimizing downtime and service disruption.

Change management is another area where BGP automation provides significant benefits. Automated configuration management tools enable operators to test BGP policy changes in staging environments or virtual labs before applying them to production routers. This practice reduces the likelihood of introducing routing loops, policy conflicts, or service outages. Additionally, automation frameworks can enforce role-based access control and maintain an auditable record of all BGP-related changes, supporting regulatory compliance and simplifying post-change troubleshooting.

Version control systems like Git have become integral to network automation workflows, allowing teams to track, review, and roll back BGP configuration changes as needed. With GitOps methodologies, network teams can implement continuous integration and continuous deployment (CI/CD) pipelines for BGP configurations, applying the same principles used in software development to network infrastructure. By automating the process of merging approved configuration changes into production networks, organizations can achieve faster and safer deployments.

Automation is also critical in multi-vendor environments where routers and switches from different manufacturers coexist. By using open standards such as NETCONF, RESTCONF, or OpenConfig, operators can automate BGP configurations and operations across diverse devices without being tied to vendor-specific CLI syntax. This interoperability streamlines the management of complex networks and facilitates smoother transitions between hardware platforms or software versions.

In service provider networks, BGP automation simplifies the provisioning of customer services. When new customer connections are established, automation tools can automatically configure BGP sessions, apply customer-specific route filters, and allocate VPNv4 or VPNv6 address families for MPLS Layer 3 VPNs. Automation reduces customer onboarding times, ensures consistent service delivery, and improves the overall customer experience.

The adoption of automation also helps address the growing skills gap in network operations. By codifying best practices and operational expertise into automated workflows, organizations can reduce their reliance on manual tasks and ensure that even junior engineers can manage complex BGP deployments confidently. Automation abstracts many of the repetitive and error-prone aspects of BGP management, freeing up skilled engineers to focus on higher-value activities, such as network design and optimization.

As networks evolve to support 5G, edge computing, and cloud-native applications, the demand for automation in BGP operations will continue to rise. The combination of BGP's scalability and flexibility with automation's efficiency and consistency enables organizations to build networks that are resilient, agile, and ready to meet the demands of modern digital services. Whether in service provider backbones, enterprise WANs, or hyperscale cloud environments, BGP automation is now a cornerstone of operational excellence and a critical enabler of scalable, secure, and high-performing networks.

Open Source BGP Implementations

The Border Gateway Protocol has long been associated with commercial routers and proprietary network operating systems, but the growing adoption of open networking and the open-source movement has brought several high-quality open-source BGP implementations to the forefront. These implementations provide network operators, researchers, and enterprises with flexible and cost-effective alternatives to traditional vendor-supplied routing stacks. Open-source BGP daemons enable organizations to deploy routing solutions on commodity hardware, virtual machines, and containers while maintaining full control over the routing software stack and its features. Over the years, several open-source projects have matured to the point where they now power critical production networks, large-scale research environments, and next-generation software-defined infrastructures.

One of the most widely adopted open-source BGP implementations is FRRouting, also known as FRR. Derived from the earlier Quagga project, FRRouting has become a go-to choice for organizations seeking a robust and actively maintained routing suite. FRR supports multiple routing protocols, including BGP, OSPF, IS-IS, and RIP, making it a versatile option for both service providers and enterprises. Its modular design and rich feature set include support for BGP multiprotocol extensions, route reflectors, BGP-LS, BGP FlowSpec, and segment routing. FRR's CLI is modeled closely after traditional network operating systems, which eases the learning curve for engineers transitioning from proprietary platforms.

FRRouting is particularly popular in modern data center and cloud environments, where it is often deployed on white-box switches and Linux-based virtual machines. When combined with automation tools and Linux networking features such as network namespaces and VRFs, FRR enables highly customized routing setups that can rival traditional hardware routers. Its integration with orchestration platforms like Kubernetes and container networking solutions, such as Calico or Cilium, also makes FRR a preferred choice for enabling BGP-based service advertisement in cloud-native environments.

Another prominent open-source BGP implementation is BIRD (BIRD Internet Routing Daemon). BIRD is widely used by Internet service providers, Internet exchange points, and academic networks due to its scalability and configuration flexibility. BIRD supports both IPv4 and IPv6 routing tables and provides powerful policy controls through its configuration language, allowing operators to fine-tune route import and export policies. BIRD excels in route server deployments, particularly at IXPs, where stability, low resource consumption, and high route-processing performance are paramount. Many IXPs, including large ones like DE-CIX and LINX, rely on BIRD to operate their route servers, supporting multilateral peering relationships between hundreds of autonomous systems.

One of BIRD's strengths is its ability to maintain separate routing tables for different address families or policy domains. This makes it particularly well-suited for advanced applications such as BGP communities filtering, RPKI validation integration, and hybrid IPv4/IPv6 peering environments. Despite its lightweight footprint, BIRD has proven capable of handling full Internet routing tables with ease, making it a popular option for Tier 2 and Tier 3 service providers seeking open-source alternatives.

GoBGP is a more recent addition to the ecosystem, written in the Go programming language and designed with modern software architecture principles in mind. GoBGP is focused on providing an extensible and developer-friendly BGP implementation, featuring a clean API-driven approach that simplifies integration with SDN controllers, automation platforms, and microservices-based architectures. GoBGP supports many of the advanced BGP capabilities found in more mature projects, including multiprotocol extensions, route reflection, EVPN, and FlowSpec. Its gRPC-based API makes it ideal for network engineers and developers seeking to build custom network automation or telemetry solutions.

The flexibility of GoBGP has led to its adoption in several research and production environments, particularly where agile deployment and integration with external systems are essential. For example, GoBGP is often used in projects where dynamic policy injection, on-demand route advertisement, or real-time route monitoring are required. Its modular design and native API support position it as a compelling choice for organizations building programmable or intent-based networking systems.

OpenBGPD, developed by the OpenBSD project, is another open-source BGP implementation that emphasizes security and simplicity. While OpenBGPD may not have as extensive a feature set as FRR or BIRD, it is highly regarded for its clean codebase and strong focus on secure programming practices. It provides a streamlined and reliable BGP implementation, suitable for organizations prioritizing minimalism and security. OpenBGPD is often favored in firewall platforms, network appliances, and minimalist Linux or BSD-based routing environments.

The open-source nature of these BGP implementations offers several operational advantages. First and foremost, organizations have full access to the source code, enabling them to audit the software for security vulnerabilities, customize functionality, or contribute new features back to the community. This level of transparency and control is particularly valuable in security-conscious industries such as finance, government, and critical infrastructure.

Open-source BGP daemons also foster innovation by making it easier for researchers and network engineers to experiment with novel routing concepts, develop new protocol extensions, or build custom traffic engineering solutions. For example, network operators can implement specialized BGP policies or integrate BGP directly into custom SDN controllers using the APIs provided by projects like GoBGP or FRR.

The flexibility provided by open-source routing stacks extends to deployment models as well. These BGP daemons can run on physical servers, virtual machines, or within containerized environments. This allows organizations to deploy virtual routers for testing, lab environments, or production use cases without being tied to specific hardware platforms. Open-source BGP implementations have been widely adopted in modern service provider networks, cloud infrastructure, and even at the network edge, where lightweight BGP speakers are needed to exchange routes with upstream providers or customers.

Despite their many benefits, open-source BGP solutions must be deployed with careful consideration of operational requirements, especially in high-throughput production environments. While many open-source implementations are capable of handling full BGP routing tables and large-scale peerings, tuning, monitoring, and capacity planning are essential to ensure performance and stability. Integrating these daemons with established monitoring tools, logging systems, and automation frameworks helps ensure consistent operations and rapid response to routing anomalies.

The increasing popularity of open-source BGP implementations reflects a broader trend toward open networking and disaggregation, where network operators seek greater flexibility and control over their infrastructure. As more organizations transition away from vertically integrated vendor solutions to software-driven networking architectures, open-source BGP stacks are poised to play an even larger role in shaping the future of global Internet routing and next-generation network designs.

Vendor-Specific BGP Features

While the Border Gateway Protocol is a standards-based protocol defined by a series of RFCs, network equipment vendors often implement additional proprietary features to enhance BGP's functionality, improve performance, or provide better integration with their specific platforms. These vendor-specific BGP extensions are designed to address unique operational needs and offer competitive differentiation. Although these features are not universally supported, they can provide valuable capabilities for network operators who rely on a particular vendor's ecosystem. Understanding these proprietary enhancements is critical when designing multi-vendor networks, as interoperability may be affected if vendor-specific features are enabled on one side but not supported by peers.

Cisco Systems, one of the leading network equipment vendors, has introduced several proprietary BGP features over the years. One well-known enhancement is Cisco's Conditional Route Injection (CRI), which allows routes to be automatically injected into the BGP routing table based on the presence or absence of specific trigger routes. This feature enables dynamic routing adjustments without manual intervention, helping operators implement highly responsive routing policies. Cisco also supports the BGP PIC (Prefix Independent Convergence) feature, designed to accelerate convergence in MPLS and IP networks. BGP PIC reduces convergence time after a link or node failure by pre-computing backup paths and installing them into the forwarding information base, enabling fast reroute capabilities even in large-scale networks.

Cisco routers also offer BGP Dynamic Update Peer-Groups, a feature that enhances scalability by enabling peer groups to be formed dynamically based on common session characteristics. This reduces the amount of memory and CPU resources required to manage large numbers of BGP sessions, making it ideal for service provider networks with hundreds or thousands of peers. In addition, Cisco's BGP Route Dampening enhancements allow operators to fine-tune suppression parameters beyond the baseline RFC specifications, giving more granular control over route flap dampening policies.

Juniper Networks, another major player in the routing space, offers its own set of BGP extensions through its Junos operating system. Juniper's BGP multipath load balancing capabilities are particularly noteworthy, as they allow for the installation of multiple BGP paths into the routing table and enable equal-cost multipath (ECMP) forwarding at scale. Juniper also supports diverse BGP policy framework capabilities with its Junos routing policy language, enabling complex conditional statements and policy chains that provide unparalleled flexibility in shaping routing behavior.

A unique feature found in Juniper routers is the ability to configure BGP add-path with path selection policies, which allows multiple paths for the same prefix to be advertised to peers. This is particularly useful in scenarios where route reflectors are deployed, as it reduces the risk of suboptimal routing or path hiding within the iBGP mesh. Juniper's implementation also supports advanced damping mechanisms, where operators can apply flap dampening policies selectively based on peer groups or communities, enhancing route stability while preserving necessary flexibility.

Arista Networks, a leader in cloud and data center networking, has integrated BGP deeply into its EOS (Extensible Operating System) architecture. Arista offers CloudVision, an orchestration and automation platform that leverages BGP EVPN (Ethernet VPN) for data center interconnects and VXLAN overlays. Arista's implementation focuses on seamless integration of BGP with virtualized workloads and cloud-native environments, offering features such as EVPN Type-5 route propagation and EVPN route servers to simplify multi-tenant data center fabrics.

Arista also provides enhancements around BGP peer monitoring and analytics, leveraging EOS's state streaming capabilities. Network telemetry data, including BGP session metrics, route updates, and policy compliance information, can be streamed to analytics platforms in real-time. This allows operators to proactively monitor BGP health and detect anomalies before they impact services. Additionally, Arista's EOS supports native API access, enabling programmatic control over BGP sessions, route policies, and route dampening behavior.

Huawei, a major global networking vendor, has introduced several proprietary BGP features within its VRP (Versatile Routing Platform) software. Huawei routers support enhanced GR (Graceful Restart) mechanisms for BGP sessions, allowing faster convergence and service continuity during planned maintenance or software upgrades. Huawei also provides advanced hierarchical BGP configurations, enabling operators to segment their BGP policies across multiple layers of peer groups and address families, providing refined control over route distribution in complex multi-region networks.

Huawei's VRP also includes support for BGP-based VPN technologies beyond standard MPLS L3VPNs, such as Seamless MPLS and BGP-based EVPN for L2 and L3 services. Operators using Huawei equipment can leverage these proprietary extensions to deploy integrated solutions for enterprise VPNs, carrier Ethernet, and data center interconnects. Huawei has also invested heavily in supporting advanced BGP FlowSpec implementations for DDoS mitigation, allowing for distributed attack detection and automated threat response across multiple routers.

Extreme Networks offers proprietary BGP features tailored to campus and enterprise networks. One such feature is Extreme's Fabric Attach, which uses BGP to integrate with network fabric technologies for simplified service provisioning and automated VLAN attachment. Extreme routers also support enhanced BGP dampening and local-pref adjustment capabilities that work in tandem with their centralized management platform, ExtremeCloud IQ, streamlining network management in large distributed environments.

In addition to proprietary features provided by major vendors, some vendors implement platform-specific optimizations aimed at improving BGP scalability and resource efficiency. For example, hardware acceleration techniques, such as BGP route processing offload to specialized ASICs, allow routers to handle larger BGP tables and faster convergence times. These hardware-assisted features are often combined with proprietary software enhancements to deliver high performance in demanding service provider and data center environments.

However, the use of vendor-specific BGP features comes with important considerations. While these features can provide significant benefits in terms of performance, automation, and flexibility, they can also create challenges when operating multi-vendor networks. Inconsistent feature support across different vendor platforms can lead to interoperability issues, particularly when proprietary extensions deviate from standard BGP behavior. Operators must carefully assess the impact of proprietary features on interoperability, especially in hybrid environments where routers from different vendors participate in the same BGP topology.

To address these challenges, many network architects adopt a hybrid approach, using vendor-specific features where they provide a clear operational advantage, while adhering to standard BGP behaviors for inter-domain or multi-vendor segments. Additionally, thorough testing in lab environments and alignment with industry best practices are essential to ensure that proprietary BGP enhancements do not introduce unforeseen complications into production networks.

Despite these caveats, vendor-specific BGP features continue to play a crucial role in meeting the diverse and evolving demands of modern network operations. Whether it is improving convergence times, simplifying traffic engineering, enhancing route policy flexibility, or integrating BGP with cloud-native platforms, these proprietary capabilities help operators maximize the potential of their chosen network infrastructure. As networks become more dynamic and distributed, vendor-specific BGP innovations will remain an important toolset in the ongoing quest to optimize and secure large-scale routing environments.

The Future of BGP

The Border Gateway Protocol has been the backbone of inter-domain routing for over three decades, enabling autonomous systems to exchange reachability information and construct the global Internet as we know it today. Despite its resilience and adaptability, BGP faces growing challenges and scrutiny as the Internet continues to evolve. The rapid proliferation of cloud computing, mobile networks, content delivery platforms, and new technologies such as 5G and IoT are reshaping the demands placed on the routing system. In response, researchers, standards bodies, and network operators are exploring ways to modernize BGP to meet the future needs of an ever-expanding digital ecosystem.

One of the most pressing issues that BGP must address is security. While BGP was originally designed in an era when trust among network operators was implicit, today's Internet faces a constant threat of route hijacks, leaks, and other forms of misconfigurations or attacks. Efforts such as the Resource Public Key Infrastructure have already introduced origin validation mechanisms to mitigate the risks of prefix hijacking. However, the adoption of RPKI is not yet universal, and challenges remain in achieving global deployment. In addition to origin validation, the community has been developing BGPsec, a cryptographic extension designed to secure the AS_PATH attribute by providing path validation. While BGPsec promises a more secure routing environment, its operational complexity, computational overhead, and limited deployment so far present obstacles that will need to be overcome for it to become a widely accepted standard.

Scalability is another key concern shaping the future of BGP. The growth of the global routing table continues unabated, driven by factors such as de-aggregation of prefixes, expansion of IPv6, and the proliferation of new autonomous systems. While modern routers have become more capable of handling millions of routes, the increase in routing information also results in longer convergence times and higher resource consumption. Efforts to improve scalability focus on both technical and operational strategies. Technologies like Segment Routing and Service Function Chaining aim to reduce the reliance on per-flow state in the core of the network, offloading complexity to the edges. Meanwhile, there is a growing emphasis on aggressive route aggregation, network automation, and optimization of route reflector designs to ensure that BGP can scale in line with global network demands.

The future of BGP is also closely linked to the rise of intent-based networking and automation. As networks become increasingly software-defined and automated, there is a push to integrate BGP more deeply into programmable frameworks. BGP's adaptability has already allowed it to evolve from a simple path-vector protocol to a control plane component in modern data centers, cloud networks, and SDN environments. The next phase of evolution will likely see BGP become more tightly integrated with orchestration platforms and telemetry systems, enabling networks to react autonomously to changing conditions. For example, BGP policies could be dynamically adjusted in response to telemetry data indicating congestion, latency, or link degradation, without human intervention.

Artificial intelligence and machine learning are also poised to influence BGP's trajectory. As network operators adopt AI-driven platforms for anomaly detection, predictive maintenance, and traffic engineering, BGP will serve as a critical control plane mechanism for implementing these recommendations. AI-assisted routing optimization could help networks make more intelligent routing decisions, dynamically adjust route attributes, and mitigate threats such as route leaks or hijacks in near real-time. This integration will require BGP to interface more seamlessly with automation pipelines and analytics engines, fostering a new era of autonomous and self-healing networks.

The increasing decentralization of Internet services through edge computing, IoT, and 5G networks presents additional considerations for BGP's future role. Edge computing introduces more localized networks closer to end-users, requiring BGP to operate effectively in environments with a larger number of smaller, distributed nodes. This trend could lead to changes in how BGP is deployed, with a stronger focus on lightweight implementations, fast convergence, and optimized routing policies tailored for edge networks. BGP will need to adapt to these more fragmented topologies while still maintaining its role in aggregating and distributing reachability information across the broader Internet.

Another emerging aspect of BGP's future is its role in supporting multi-cloud connectivity. Enterprises increasingly rely on multiple cloud providers for redundancy, flexibility, and cost optimization. BGP facilitates direct interconnections between private networks and cloud platforms, making it a key enabler of hybrid and multi-cloud architectures. To support these evolving environments, cloud providers are extending BGP capabilities with features like BGP-based service discovery, cloud-native route reflectors, and API-driven BGP configuration interfaces. This tighter integration will position BGP as a critical component of enterprise cloud strategies, requiring continued enhancements to its flexibility and ease of automation.

The evolution of BGP is not occurring in isolation but rather as part of broader efforts to enhance the reliability and security of the Internet's core infrastructure. Initiatives like MANRS (Mutually Agreed Norms for Routing Security) are driving operational improvements by encouraging network operators to adopt best practices related to filtering, anti-spoofing, and routing security. BGP's future will undoubtedly be shaped by how widely these practices are adopted and how well they are supported by new BGP implementations and features.

Another area where BGP may see further development is in multicast and service-layer routing. Although unicast routing has long been BGP's primary role, there is a growing interest in using BGP as a control plane for multicast VPNs, service chains, and network slicing in 5G architectures. These evolving use cases may lead to the introduction of new BGP address families, attributes, and policy extensions designed to support emerging services and applications with greater flexibility and granularity.

Ultimately, the future of BGP will be shaped by the balance between preserving its core functionality and adapting to the Internet's changing landscape. While BGP has stood the test of time as a simple yet powerful protocol, it must continue evolving to meet the challenges posed by an increasingly complex, dynamic, and security-conscious world. Through a combination of technical innovations, community-driven best practices, and tighter integration with automation and orchestration platforms, BGP is likely to remain the foundational protocol for inter-domain routing well into the future, supporting the next generation of global digital infrastructure.

Regulatory and Compliance Considerations

The Border Gateway Protocol plays a critical role in the operation of the global Internet, making it a focal point in discussions surrounding regulatory compliance, legal frameworks, and operational best practices. As the Internet has become an indispensable part of modern economies and national infrastructures, governments and regulatory bodies have increasingly scrutinized how networks manage BGP operations, particularly in areas such as security, data sovereignty, critical infrastructure protection, and privacy. For network operators, service providers, and enterprises running BGP, understanding and adhering to regulatory and compliance considerations has become essential to ensure the integrity and resilience of their routing infrastructure.

A major regulatory concern is the security of BGP and its susceptibility to routing leaks, hijacks, and other malicious or accidental disruptions. In response, international efforts such as the MANRS (Mutually Agreed Norms for Routing Security) initiative have emerged to establish baseline routing security practices. MANRS encourages network operators to adopt measures like filtering invalid routes, implementing anti-spoofing controls, and promoting the adoption of RPKI for route origin validation. While MANRS is a voluntary framework, several regulators and industry groups worldwide now view compliance with its principles as an essential component of responsible network operations, particularly for operators that form part of critical national infrastructure.

In regions where network infrastructure is classified as critical to national security, governments are increasingly imposing specific requirements on BGP operations. These requirements may include mandatory participation in national-level incident response exercises, strict adherence to route filtering policies, and the implementation of monitoring and alerting systems capable of detecting abnormal BGP events. Regulatory bodies often expect operators of critical networks, such as those supporting emergency services, defense, finance, and utilities, to demonstrate that they can detect and mitigate route leaks and hijacks promptly.

Another key regulatory topic is data sovereignty, which concerns where and how data is routed across borders. In jurisdictions with strict data residency laws, network operators must ensure that data originating from within a country or region does not inadvertently traverse foreign networks or jurisdictions without proper authorization. While BGP itself does not provide direct control over data paths at the application level, routing decisions influenced by BGP can determine which countries or regions traffic passes through. As a result, regulators may require network operators to implement traffic engineering policies that prioritize domestic or in-region transit routes, ensuring that sensitive data remains within compliant geographic boundaries.

In addition to data sovereignty, privacy regulations such as the General Data Protection Regulation in the European Union emphasize the importance of protecting user data, including metadata about routing and traffic flows. Although BGP is primarily concerned with network-level information rather than user-level data, improper configuration or exposure of BGP policies could potentially reveal sensitive operational details about a network's internal structure or interconnection relationships. Regulatory frameworks increasingly expect operators to treat BGP data as part of their broader network security and privacy obligations, applying appropriate access controls and limiting exposure of sensitive routing information.

For multinational enterprises and cloud service providers, regulatory compliance also extends to BGP policies that govern hybrid and multi-cloud connectivity. Enterprises connecting to public cloud platforms via BGP-based direct connect services must ensure that their routing policies comply with industry-specific regulations, such as financial sector guidelines or healthcare privacy rules. This includes validating that BGP filters are in place to prevent the propagation of unauthorized or non-compliant prefixes between on-premises networks, cloud environments, and third-party partners.

Interconnection agreements between autonomous systems increasingly reference regulatory requirements as part of contractual obligations. When two networks establish a peering relationship, they often agree to adhere to certain security and routing practices, including compliance with national regulations, industry frameworks like MANRS, or even specific clauses related to lawful intercept capabilities. Failure to comply with these obligations can expose network operators to legal liabilities, penalties, or reputational harm, particularly if a BGP-related incident leads to service disruption or data exposure.

Compliance also intersects with incident reporting requirements in many regulatory regimes. Several countries now mandate that operators report BGP anomalies, such as route leaks or hijacks, to national cybersecurity centers or telecommunications regulators. Timely reporting enables authorities to assess the potential impact of routing incidents on public safety, financial systems, or critical infrastructure, and to coordinate an appropriate response. For this reason, network operators must have robust incident detection and escalation procedures integrated into their BGP monitoring frameworks.

Audits and compliance assessments frequently include reviews of BGP configurations and routing practices. Regulatory bodies or independent auditors may request evidence of proper route filtering, secure peering arrangements, documented routing policies, and participation in routing security initiatives. Demonstrating compliance requires operators to maintain detailed records of BGP policies, filtering rules, and change management logs. Automation and configuration management systems that track BGP-related changes can play a key role in helping organizations meet audit requirements and ensure ongoing compliance.

In recent years, regulators have also expressed concerns about the centralization of Internet routing control, particularly with the concentration of global Internet traffic through a limited number of transit providers or geographic regions. Discussions around network neutrality and fair access have touched on the role of BGP in determining traffic paths and influencing the economics of interconnection. While BGP itself is policy-neutral, operators must navigate regulatory expectations around non-discriminatory traffic routing, particularly when providing services to customers in regulated industries or public sector organizations.

To meet evolving compliance requirements, many network operators have integrated BGP security and policy controls into their broader risk management and governance frameworks. This often includes regular policy reviews, adoption of best practices such as RPKI and BGP FlowSpec, and participation in industry forums focused on routing security. Additionally, cross-functional collaboration between network engineering teams, legal departments, and compliance officers is critical to ensuring that BGP operations align with regulatory obligations and do not inadvertently introduce risks.

Looking ahead, regulatory frameworks will likely place even greater emphasis on BGP security, resilience, and transparency. Emerging guidelines from bodies such as the European Union Agency for Cybersecurity and national regulators increasingly call for the adoption of cryptographic mechanisms like BGPsec, mandatory origin validation, and coordinated incident response capabilities. As governments seek to strengthen the security of global Internet infrastructure, BGP operations will remain a focal point for compliance efforts across industries and regions.

For organizations operating in multiple jurisdictions, balancing regulatory requirements with operational efficiency and business goals will continue to shape BGP deployment strategies. While compliance may introduce additional complexities, it also drives the adoption of more secure, resilient, and well-managed routing practices, ultimately benefiting both individual networks and the global Internet ecosystem as a whole.

BGP and the Global Routing Table

The global routing table is the foundation of the Internet's ability to deliver data between billions of devices, and the Border Gateway Protocol is the mechanism that enables this massive system to function. The global routing table, also known as the Default-Free

Zone (DFZ) routing table, is the collection of all routes that autonomous systems exchange to enable end-to-end reachability across the Internet. BGP serves as the protocol that stitches together all of these individual networks into a seamless whole. Each autonomous system contributes prefixes to this table, advertising to its neighbors the IP address blocks it can deliver traffic to. Over the years, as the Internet has expanded, so too has the global routing table, which now contains over one million IPv4 prefixes and continues to grow steadily as IPv6 adoption increases.

The rapid growth of the global routing table has been driven by several key factors. First, the sheer proliferation of networks, devices, and services has resulted in a corresponding rise in the number of IP prefixes being advertised. Enterprises, service providers, and content delivery networks all inject their IP address blocks into the BGP ecosystem, contributing to the size of the table. Moreover, the widespread practice of de-aggregation, where organizations announce smaller, more specific prefixes instead of aggregating them into larger summaries, has further inflated the table. De-aggregation often occurs for traffic engineering purposes, as operators seek more control over how traffic enters or exits their networks. While this provides flexibility at the operational level, it places additional strain on the global routing table.

The global routing table's size has critical implications for the performance and scalability of the Internet. Every router in the DFZ must maintain a complete view of this table to make forwarding decisions for packets traversing autonomous system boundaries. As the table grows, so too does the demand on router memory, CPU, and forwarding plane resources. Older routers with limited TCAM (Ternary Content-Addressable Memory) or other hardware constraints may struggle to accommodate the full table, leading to routing instability or service degradation. Consequently, the continuous expansion of the global routing table has driven operators to invest in more capable hardware and has influenced network design considerations globally.

BGP is uniquely suited to managing this complex and expansive routing system because of its policy-based and path-vector nature. Unlike link-state protocols that require complete topological knowledge, BGP exchanges only reachability information and associated attributes, such as AS_PATH, NEXT_HOP, and LOCAL_PREF, allowing routers to select the most appropriate routes based on local policies. This flexibility enables operators to prioritize certain routes, avoid undesirable transit providers, or shape traffic flows to optimize performance and cost. At the same time, BGP's ability to selectively filter prefixes prevents networks from accepting unnecessary or malicious route advertisements, helping to manage the growth and integrity of the global routing table.

A critical aspect of managing the global routing table is the practice of route filtering and prefix-list enforcement. Most operators implement ingress and egress filtering policies to control which prefixes are accepted from or advertised to peers. This not only limits the propagation of unnecessary de-aggregated routes but also serves as a safeguard against misconfigurations and potential attacks, such as route leaks or hijacks. The deployment of filtering mechanisms like maximum prefix limits further protects routers by automatically shutting down BGP sessions if an excessive number of prefixes are received from a peer, preventing memory exhaustion and routing instability.

The global routing table is also directly impacted by the transition to IPv6. Although IPv6 adoption has been slower than originally anticipated, it has seen consistent growth, and IPv6 prefixes now represent a significant and growing portion of the routing table. Unlike IPv4, where address scarcity has led to tight aggregation of address space, the abundance of IPv6 addresses encourages more granular subnetting. This has the potential to accelerate the growth of the IPv6 global routing table. Operators must therefore manage both IPv4 and IPv6 tables simultaneously, further increasing the resource demands on routing infrastructure.

BGP's role in maintaining the global routing table also involves the use of route reflectors and confederations to scale iBGP environments. As large autonomous systems, such as Tier 1 service providers, maintain multiple border routers that peer with the DFZ, internal mechanisms are needed to distribute the full routing table within the AS. Route reflectors help reduce the number of iBGP sessions required while ensuring that routers have the complete view of the Internet's routing topology. However, improper route reflector configurations or insufficient filtering at route reflectors can exacerbate routing issues and contribute to instability in the DFZ.

The importance of routing table hygiene cannot be overstated. Best practices such as prefix aggregation, the implementation of BGP communities for route control, and the adoption of RPKI to validate route origins are critical for sustaining a manageable and secure global routing table. While these techniques help control table growth and improve route validity, they require coordinated efforts across thousands of network operators worldwide.

BGP monitoring and telemetry tools have become indispensable in managing the global routing table. Operators rely on route collectors, looking glass servers, and telemetry platforms to analyze table size trends, track anomalies, and monitor BGP update churn. BGP churn, the rate at which route advertisements and withdrawals occur, can spike during network failures or misconfigurations, placing additional strain on routers and exacerbating convergence delays. Understanding and mitigating factors that contribute to excessive churn is essential for maintaining Internet stability.

The evolution of the global routing table reflects both the success and the challenges of the Internet's distributed nature. As more regions, service providers, and networks join the global ecosystem, the routing table will continue to grow. Balancing the need for routing granularity with the imperative to keep the table scalable is a delicate task that requires collaboration among operators, standards bodies, and technology vendors. Despite the challenges, BGP remains the fundamental protocol that enables the global routing table to function effectively, providing the connective tissue for the world's autonomous systems and ensuring that data can flow reliably across borders and between continents.

BGP in Satellite and Edge Networks

The expansion of satellite communications and edge computing has introduced new complexities and opportunities for the application of the Border Gateway Protocol. Traditionally, BGP has been the backbone of terrestrial inter-domain routing, connecting autonomous systems across data centers, service providers, and the broader Internet. However, as organizations push network functions closer to users and extend connectivity to remote and underserved regions through satellite links, BGP's role has become increasingly important in these non-traditional environments. Both satellite and edge networks require robust and adaptive routing strategies to manage unique constraints such as high latency, limited bandwidth, intermittent connectivity, and diverse topologies.

In satellite networks, BGP is often used to manage routing between ground stations, satellite gateways, and terrestrial networks. With the rise of Low Earth Orbit (LEO) satellite constellations, such as those deployed by providers like Starlink and OneWeb, satellite networks have become more dynamic than their Geostationary Orbit (GEO) predecessors. LEO satellites move relative to the Earth's surface, requiring frequent handoffs and dynamic path changes as users switch between satellites or ground stations. In this context, BGP serves as a critical component for announcing reachable prefixes from remote satellite terminals to the terrestrial backbone and vice versa. BGP's ability to scale across distributed networks and maintain route stability in the face of link variability makes it well-suited for the unique demands of satellite networking.

A key challenge in satellite BGP deployments is dealing with the inherent latency introduced by satellite hops, particularly in GEO systems where round-trip times often exceed 500 milliseconds. This latency can affect BGP convergence times, especially during failover scenarios or when session resets occur due to link degradation. To address these issues, operators often employ BGP timers tuned for longer hold and keepalive intervals to accommodate the increased round-trip times. Additionally, route reflectors are frequently used within satellite backbones to centralize route dissemination and minimize the number of BGP sessions needed across constrained satellite links, reducing overhead and optimizing resource usage.

In LEO satellite systems, the network behaves more like a terrestrial mobile network, with frequent topological changes as satellites orbit and users dynamically switch between ground stations. BGP in these environments must be highly responsive, often augmented by automation and orchestration systems that can adjust BGP policies in real time based on satellite visibility and link availability. For instance, an edge node in a remote region may receive prefixes from multiple LEO satellites, and BGP path selection algorithms are used to determine the optimal route back to the terrestrial Internet, factoring in latency, bandwidth availability, and link stability.

BGP's role in satellite networks is further enhanced by its ability to support traffic engineering through the manipulation of attributes such as LOCAL_PREF and AS_PATH prepending. Operators can use these attributes to influence how traffic enters or exits the satellite network, preferring certain satellite gateways or terrestrial points of presence based on real-time conditions or cost considerations. In hybrid networks where terrestrial fiber connections are used in conjunction with satellite backhaul, BGP enables seamless route selection between the two transport options, ensuring that traffic follows the most efficient or cost-effective path available.

The application of BGP in edge networks is equally significant. Edge computing aims to bring processing, storage, and networking resources closer to end-users and devices, reducing latency and enabling real-time applications such as IoT, autonomous vehicles, and augmented reality. In edge environments, BGP is used to manage routing between edge data centers, micro data centers, and local access networks. Unlike traditional core networks, edge networks often have distributed and hierarchical topologies, with multiple layers of edge nodes aggregating traffic before handing it off to regional or core networks.

BGP's policy-driven nature makes it well-suited for these distributed edge environments. By using BGP communities and routing policies, operators can enforce locality-aware routing, ensuring that traffic between users and applications stays within the edge domain whenever possible. This reduces the dependency on centralized data centers, lowers backbone bandwidth consumption, and improves application performance. For example, in a smart city deployment, edge routers using BGP may advertise local services such as traffic management or public safety systems only to nearby nodes, preventing unnecessary traffic from traversing the core network.

The rise of 5G networks has also accelerated the adoption of BGP at the edge. Mobile operators are deploying multi-access edge computing (MEC) nodes close to radio access networks to enable ultra-low-latency services. BGP is leveraged to manage routing between MEC platforms, mobile packet cores, and the broader IP backbone. In some cases, BGP is integrated directly into virtualized network functions (VNFs) or containerized network functions (CNFs) running on edge compute nodes, enabling highly dynamic service chaining and traffic steering.

Edge networks often face operational challenges related to resource constraints, such as limited compute capacity, power availability, and network bandwidth. BGP's flexibility in scaling to lightweight, software-based routers deployed on commodity hardware makes it a practical choice for edge nodes. Open-source BGP implementations like FRRouting or BIRD are frequently used to provide routing functionality in these environments, allowing for agile deployment and easy integration with automation frameworks.

Intermittent connectivity is another common scenario in both satellite and edge networks. In remote or mobile environments, links may go up and down due to environmental conditions, mobility, or infrastructure limitations. BGP's inherent ability to adapt to changing network conditions ensures that routes are withdrawn and re-advertised efficiently when links become available or fail. However, operators must also implement damping mechanisms and conservative route flap thresholds to prevent instability caused by frequent session resets or transient link failures.

Finally, the combination of BGP with SD-WAN and overlay technologies is becoming increasingly prevalent in edge and satellite networks. Many SD-WAN solutions use BGP to integrate overlay and underlay routing domains, enabling enterprises to seamlessly extend their WANs to include satellite links and edge locations. BGP provides the policy granularity needed to control how application traffic is directed over different transport networks based on business requirements, performance metrics, or regulatory constraints.

As satellite and edge networks continue to expand to meet the demands of emerging technologies and remote connectivity needs, BGP's adaptability, scalability, and policy-driven architecture will remain indispensable. Whether enabling remote rural broadband through LEO satellites or supporting real-time industrial applications at the network edge, BGP ensures that routing decisions are optimized to meet the unique operational characteristics of these increasingly vital segments of global network infrastructure.

The Unseen Backbone: BGP and Everyday Life

The Border Gateway Protocol operates quietly in the background of the digital world, yet it is responsible for ensuring that nearly every online interaction happens smoothly. Despite its critical role, most people are unaware of BGP and how deeply it is woven into the fabric of their daily routines. From reading emails and streaming video to conducting financial transactions or working remotely, BGP silently enables seamless communication between networks spread across the globe. Without BGP, the Internet would not function as a cohesive entity, but rather as disconnected islands of information.

When an individual opens a web browser to visit a news site or an online store, their request must traverse several autonomous systems, each controlled by different Internet service providers, cloud providers, or backbone carriers. BGP determines how this traffic finds its way from the user's home network, through their ISP, across multiple upstream networks, and ultimately to the destination server. It is BGP that helps select the most efficient or available path for these packets, balancing factors like network reachability, policy preferences, and physical distance. The routing decision, while invisible to the user, directly affects the performance and reliability of their Internet experience.

Streaming services are one of the most tangible examples of how BGP impacts everyday life. When a person watches a movie or live sports event, the video content is typically delivered via a content delivery network with edge servers located close to the user. These edge nodes announce their IP prefixes using BGP to local ISPs, making the content accessible through the shortest or most optimal path. BGP ensures that high-definition video streams can be delivered with minimal buffering and reduced latency by steering user traffic to nearby servers rather than distant data centers. Without BGP's ability to optimize routing decisions, streaming services would suffer from delays, degraded quality, and outages, especially during peak usage times.

The impact of BGP extends into financial services and online transactions. Each time someone makes an online payment, transfers money between bank accounts, or accesses their online banking portal, BGP is involved in delivering the network traffic to the appropriate data centers. Banks and financial institutions rely on highly redundant and secure network architectures where BGP plays a pivotal role in providing failover paths and ensuring that critical services remain accessible even during disruptions. If a fiber cut or outage occurs along a primary route, BGP automatically reroutes traffic via alternative paths, preventing delays in payment processing or interruptions in financial services.

The pandemic era has highlighted BGP's importance in supporting remote work and virtual collaboration. The surge in video conferencing, cloud-based applications, and virtual desktops has increased the reliance on robust and efficient routing. As employees connect to corporate networks from various locations, BGP facilitates connectivity between remote users, cloud services, and private data centers. VPN connections, SaaS applications, and remote access platforms all depend on BGP to find optimal routes, avoiding congested or unstable network paths and ensuring that business operations can continue without disruption.

Online gaming is another sphere where BGP silently shapes user experiences. Gamers expect low latency and stable connections to gaming servers that may be located in regional data centers or cloud environments. BGP influences which servers a player connects to, often in coordination with Anycast routing or traffic engineering policies implemented by gaming companies. If BGP fails to optimize routing, players may experience lag, packet loss, or server disconnections, directly impacting gameplay. Game developers and network engineers work behind the scenes, constantly monitoring BGP route selection and updating policies to minimize such disruptions.

E-commerce and logistics depend heavily on BGP to keep supply chains moving and online marketplaces running smoothly. When consumers place an order through an online store, backend systems such as inventory databases, payment gateways, and fulfillment platforms must communicate across different networks. BGP ensures that these systems remain interconnected, providing seamless shopping experiences and timely delivery of goods. Even services like shipment tracking rely on BGP to allow logistics providers to share real-time updates with customers.

Public safety and emergency services also rely on BGP for critical communications. Government agencies, healthcare providers, and first responders use secure networks to coordinate disaster response, manage public health emergencies, and provide life-saving services. These networks often include dedicated circuits and private IP spaces that are integrated into the global Internet using BGP. By ensuring that these essential services can communicate reliably with external partners and cloud platforms, BGP plays a direct role in protecting public welfare.

Behind the scenes, BGP also supports the digital services that people use passively every day. Mobile phone apps that rely on cloud-based APIs, social media platforms that deliver personalized content, and smart devices that report status updates to remote servers all depend on BGP to function. Even voice-over-IP calls and SMS messages that transit between different carriers or geographies depend on BGP to establish routes across the Internet.

Despite its vital role, BGP's complexity and decentralized nature have occasionally led to incidents that bring its importance to public attention. Events such as route leaks, prefix hijacks, or major outages caused by misconfigurations have made headlines and disrupted online services at a global scale. When these incidents occur, users may notice that their favorite websites become unreachable, payments fail to go through, or services they rely on slow to a crawl. These situations serve as stark reminders that BGP is the unseen backbone keeping the interconnected world functional.

BGP's impact on everyday life extends to the way people interact with smart homes, autonomous vehicles, and the growing Internet of

Things ecosystem. Connected devices, from thermostats to industrial sensors, depend on global connectivity to exchange data, receive updates, and provide insights. BGP ensures that these devices maintain reachability, whether communicating with local cloud edges or centralized services on the opposite side of the globe.

As the Internet becomes increasingly critical to every facet of society, the significance of BGP will only continue to grow. The silent work of BGP underpins the reliability, speed, and resilience of countless digital experiences, making it one of the most important yet least visible components of the global communications infrastructure. Whether for leisure, business, healthcare, or public safety, BGP's invisible hand is always guiding the flow of information, enabling the seamless digital interactions that define modern life.